Friends in High Places

David Traynor was born in 1966 in Merseyside and grew up in the St. Helens area. His ambition was to be a hairdresser and after attending college he qualified and with financial help from his parents opened his first salon.

As a result of hard work and a dedicated staff, including his wife Andrea, he later opened a further two shops and attracted a growing list of regular clients. His life seemed mapped out and settled.

Then his manageress asked him to make up the numbers at a Tarot party she had arranged – and his life changed from that moment.

David now gives regular public demonstrations of his remarkable gifts as a medium. He helps many people with their problems including grief. Each of his demonstrations is increasingly attended by a larger following of those seeking help and reassurance. David's reward is the gratitude of those who have been comforted and put in touch with their loved ones.

To

Wendy

FRIENDS
IN HIGH PLACES

Love & Best Wishes

David Traynor

David Traynor

◇JADE◇

Jade Publishing Limited,

5 Leefields Close, Uppermill, Oldham, Lancashire, OL3 6LA
This first impression published by Jade Publishing Limited 2005

© D. Traynor 2005
All rights reserved

ISBN 1–900734–36–2 Friends in High Places

Printed in Great Britain

Typeset by Jade Publishing Limited, Oldham, Lancashire, OL3 6LA

British Library Cataloguing in Publication Data
Traynor, David
Friends in High Places
1. Traynor, David 2. Mediums – Great Britain – Biography
I. Title
ISBN–10: 1–900734–36–2
Category: Mind, Body and Spirit

email: jade@jadepublishing.co.uk
email: davidtraynor@jadepublishing.co.uk

www.jadepublishing.co.uk

Contents

Acknowledgements

This book is dedicated to all who have helped me in my journey so far... . To Jane Blackburn, for awakening my realisation and bringing me face to face with my gift; to Jim Roe, for his knowledge and understanding in nurturing my mediumship; to June Linn, her support has been immense throughout – a truly spiritual lady; to all my work colleagues who have seen great changes take place within me – they have been a source of support.

Andrea, my lovely wife, who never stops loving me; to Barry, my closest friend here on the Earth plane, who never gives up on me – no matter what. To my mother, Jean, who has always loved and protected me; to Jason, my guide and guardian and, indeed, to all of my helpers on the other side.

My sincere thanks to Pamela Daniels, for all her expertise in editing this, my first book.

Finally, a special thank you to all of the families who have made this book possible. God bless you all.

David Traynor
March, 2005

Illustrations

All copyrights are acknowledged and permission was sought, and granted, to reproduce the pictures shown in this work.

In addition, all the case-histories in this book have been vetted and approved by the people concerned except where we no longer have contact details, due to the principals involved having moved or having passed on. We shall make corrections in any future reprint should we receive representations to do so from any person directly involved. We have, in some cases, to preserve the anonymity of those concerned, changed the names.

Cover by Baxter-Cox Design

Cover picture by Stephanie de Leng

Preface

During the Second World War my mother, brother and I moved north from London to escape the blitz. Our home was only a few miles from Fighter Command Headquarters at Bentley Priory, Stanmore. We stayed with my mother's parents in Cheshire and although a bit cramped, there were no nightly visits from German bombers or the chance of a direct hit from the later indiscriminate V1 and V2 rockets.

One of my grandmother's friends was a small woman called Mabel and she attended regularly at the Spiritualist Church. She also visited people and 'did things with cards and tea leaves'. It was a mystery to us youngsters but the grown-ups seemed quite absorbed by Mabel's abilities.

Much later, about 1989 in fact, I had decided to leave the world of advertising and become a publisher. I was introduced, by a former client, to a medium who was looking for a new publisher for her second book as she was disillusioned with her first publisher. The medium was one of the three famous Dorises. There were, at that time, Doris Stokes, Doris Collins and Doris Chamberlain. My Doris was the last named. She was a small, feisty Yorkshire lass, then aged about 86, who brooked no messing about with her discipline. The rich and famous flocked to her door – some coming especially from America – but they did as they were told in Doris's house.

Doris Chamberlain had prepared, with the help of her friend Molly, a second book called *My Two Worlds*. I found it fascinating. However, after working on her book for some months and, in the days before I had a computer, re-typing it endlessly, she took it back to give it to a journalist on the *Yorkshire Post*. I have not been able to find it listed so I presume it was not published before Doris died about five years later.

More recently, a good friend of mine, whom I shall call 'Eric', had had difficulty in coming to terms with the sudden death of his father.

We spent much time discussing death, grief and related subjects and I told him of my experiences with Doris, who was a remarkably accurate medium. She had told me the name of my grandfather, my mother – even down to her preferred spelling of her name – my grandfather's name, and during a joint sitting with my wife she had revealed something about her that I did not know. Doris said that my wife had her granny's ring. We had been married eight years then and, on leaving Doris's, when asking if that was true she confirmed that she had the ring and kept it in her jewellery box. There were many other accurate, personal details revealed which could not be explained away in the manner employed by sceptics.

My friend and I decided to go together to see a medium in the hope of her contacting (or otherwise learning of) his late father. After a very unsatisfactory sitting with a not very gifted medium, we determined on one more try. A third party offered to ask at a Spiritualist Church she attended regularly and her contact recommended David Traynor. Although only practising for two years he was described as 'brilliant'.

So we went to David's house on the appointed day. Apart from his address, we knew only his forename and he ours. He was not told the purpose of our visit – just that we had requested a sitting. When Barry opened the door I said, 'Hello, David, we're Brian and Eric. We have an appointment for six o'clock'. Barry asked us in explaining that he was not David but Barry, and that David was waiting in the conservatory.

David asked which one of us was Brian and which one Eric. He said, 'Right, I'll start with you, Brian', and promptly proceeded to astound us both with amazingly accurate details of a matter concerning a most unusual car accident. He gave names, relationships, the scene, details of the accident itself and the outcome. Eric, who was aware of the incident, sat there open-mouthed, not just at what David was relating but the accuracy of it too. So did I, as I busily scribbled verbatim notes. David did not know either of us, nor why we had come and certainly could not have had any prior knowledge of the accident, which had occurred a number years earlier in a different part of the country. Furthermore, because of my previous sittings with Doris, I made sure my answers were confined to 'Yes' and 'No'.

When Eric's turn came, there was more astounding accuracy regarding his father including his name, personal details and of his former military service and the names of his father's relatives and peers. There was a particular reference to his father having 'had two mothers' which David could not reconcile – in fact, he even apologised for the seemingly nonsensical statement and explained that he 'just gave it as it came'. Even I was not aware that Eric's father was an orphan or of the significance of what David had related until Eric explained and latterly described David's information as 'a bull's-eye'. For good measure, Eric was also given the name of his own home, its location and its former use before he had converted it. After about three hours, we came away amazed at David's abilities and, more importantly for Eric, reconciled that death is not the black hole that some would have us believe. After our disappointing experience with the first medium Eric described David as, 'The real deal! He didn't know us from Adam; in fact, we could have asked him for the window cleaning money and he would have paid us', he commented. Eric found the experience eased markedly the grief he had suffered and thereafter, he began to pick up his life's normal pace again with renewed enthusiasm and vigour.

Eric is not an 'arty' person – he is a qualified professional man of scientific persuasion and logical thought who had neither belief nor scepticism. Articulate and of lithe wit, he says simply of that night that 'we witnessed at first hand an extraordinary happening by an extraordinary man'.

Those who denigrate gifted mediums like David Traynor, do so, in my view, out of fear, ignorance, misguided religious fervour or show a distinct reluctance to approach the subject in a rational, open-minded manner.

I remember Doris Chamberlain telling me once of a priest who, not having revealed his calling, arranged a sitting with her and then began to berate her for evil-doings. Doris, who was a religious woman, took offence and defended herself stoutly and, much to his amazement, began to give the priest his life's history. Thereafter, he went to her every six months! Doris had reinforced his beliefs, for he and his church promise the after-life, called Heaven, and Doris had provided confirmation for him in a most dramatic way.

Brian Prescott,
Publisher.

April, 2005.

Chapter 1

My Early Years

I was eleven years old and scared of the dark; I always had been, so every night I relied upon the modest light of a 20watt bulb, in a bedside lamp, to keep my fears at bay. If I had been asked what I was frightened of I could not have said, for the fear was of something nameless.

I had switched on my lamp and gone to sleep as usual. In the early hours of the morning, something woke me. As I lay there, still with my eyes closed, I gradually became aware of a "presence" in my room. I was suddenly "wide" awake – but did not dare to open my eyes. I could sense something – someone – looking around my bedroom, then – Oh horror! turning its attention to me for a moment, before continuing its inspection of the surroundings. I was terrified, petrified, unable to move or breathe, sweat beginning to start from every pore. After what seemed an eternity, when I was unable even to think, I came to realize that the "thing" was not actually *doing* anything, just looking. I began to formulate a plan: it was probably a burglar. I would scream, then my parents would come in and catch him. I decided to count very slowly to three, then open my eyes...

An old man was standing by my bed looking at me, but not in a threatening way. He had a moustache and very wavy hair. He clearly wasn't a burglar because he smiled kindly at me. I began to breathe more freely. In a moment, I should doubtless have an explanation of why he was there; and then he removed his hair – it was a wig!

I tried to scream. Not a sound came out of my mouth. Next, the man began slowly to disappear – first his feet and legs, and then his top half, fading until it was gone. Panting furiously, I was at last able to emit a strangled scream, then a shout of 'Mum! Dad! Help!' No-one came to my aid. My parents' bedroom was next door to mine, so why didn't they hear me? I became aware of a sort of haze around me. It was almost as if I were enveloped in a sound-proof bubble.

The telephone suddenly rang shrilly. The haze cleared instantly. I actually felt the atmosphere return to normal, 'Mum, Dad, are you there?' I cried. 'What's the matter?' my mother called, running into my room...

I was born in St. Helens, Lancashire, in the 1960s into an ordinary, respectable, working-class Roman Catholic family, the second of two sons born to my parents. In my earliest years, before I started school, I felt confident, loved, happy and – except for my fear of the darkness – secure.

As a child I was said to be very creative, having a wonderful imagination which at the age of four was a great source of amusement in our household. I played endlessly with cardboard boxes and the uses I put them to often astounded my parents.

At the age of five, I made a piano from a tissue box – it was so well constructed and finished that my mother placed it on the sideboard in our static caravan holiday home. I can remember how proud I felt when anyone admired it.

My first year at school had been difficult. It had got off to a bad start. All my friends in the street where I lived had been accepted into St. Austin's Infants – my mother had applied for a place for me but had been too late. I, being a Roman Catholic, had to go to the next nearest Catholic school which was the Sacred Heart and, believe me, when I say I didn't want to go – I really mean that. My parents had a nightmare on their hands. For several months, they couldn't even mention the school's name in my presence.

At school I began to make friends and, in the early days, everything was "hunky dory". I had my mates at school and a gang at home, but I was sensitive. I still slept in my parents' bedroom, terrified of the dark and what the night hours might bring.

My sensitivity was beginning to be noticed by the other children; they would taunt me and towards the end of my Junior schooling, I was well known. I was often called "softy", "girly" and "sissy". I believe to this day that the majority of my tormentors didn't know what they were talking about.

Because friends were a little thin on the ground, I would take myself off to the spare room at home. It became my play room, my world where I was safe and loved. I had an imaginary friend called Maria. She was great, but she could only come along, play and talk to me when I held an ornamental brass bell, shaped like a lady in Welsh National Costume.

Day after day I would play alone. Eventually, my parents thought that as I was fond of this room, maybe it was time for me to sleep in it. Another change I didn't relish.

Being sensitive really does set you aside – and, unwittingly, children can be cruel. My problem was that I couldn't help myself. Kids would wait for me in back entries or around corners just to thump me and watch me cry, which I did on every occasion, even when they didn't hurt me.

As I look back on those traumatic years, I know now that something else was developing deep inside me.

I left the Junior school with great skill in arts and crafts, having produced a *papier maché* volcano and a rug which my mother cherished. I had also developed, during those years, the instinct of an animal – I could sense danger and avoid it. It was as if my senses went before me. I knew when people loved me and I knew the taste of hate, even at the early age of eleven. I had a very strong sense of illness and death. I often spoke to neighbours casually, as children do, and as I walked away from them, I just knew they were ill and weren't going to recover.

Then some time later, I would come home from school and Mum would break the news that so-and-so who had been ill had died. She was only telling me what I knew already.

Curiously, at the age of eleven years, I found God. You would have thought that since I was a Roman Catholic I would have found him sooner. What with religious education every day at school, assemblies four times a week and church on Sunday – well you couldn't really avoid him!

May I say at this point, one of the questions I am most frequently asked, as a medium, is have I seen God? The answer is, "No, I haven't", but my hope is that ultimately I will.

I had become friendly with a neighbour's son – Gary Pickett – a great young lad who, although he did not know it, helped me so much in my life. He attended the local Independent Methodist Church and Sunday School which were situated at the top of the street where I lived. He was involved in the Youth Club, the Sunday School Expeditions, football and parties. He was having a whale of a time.

One day he asked, 'Why don't you come? It's only five pence at the Youth Club?'

I hesitated. 'I can't, I'm a Roman Catholic', I muttered to him half-apologetically.

'Well don't let that stop you', he said. Then with a wisdom beyond his years, he asked me: 'Do you believe in God?'

'Yes,' I answered.

'That's all they want to know. Have a word with my Gran and Grandad, they help to run the church', he told me, and with that, we parted.

At no time in my life have I ever doubted the existence of God. Whether he be called God, Allah, Yahweh or Divine Spirit, I strongly believe that there is only one God and each religion leads you to Him.

If this were a universal belief, our planet would enjoy peace.

There was hell to pay in the Traynor household. I had asked if I could go to the Youth Club and Sunday School and my father refused point blank. No chance!

I was not prepared to take "no" for an answer. I cajoled, sulked became tearful, hinted that a failure to give in to my pleading might lead to serious illness on my part. I went through my entire dramatic repertoire. My mother showed signs of relenting first.

'Go on John, we'll get no peace otherwise. It will keep him off the streets.' My father knew he was beaten and so did I.

I pressed home my advantage.

In relation to the size of their faces – and compared to adults – children have large eyes. Mine were enormous; great limpid pools, and some instinct taught me to use them to effect. Placing myself directly in front of my father, so that he could not choose but notice, I turned my full gaze upon him, opening my eyes wide and arranging my mouth in such a way as to indicate supplication. My father lowered his eyes and closed them briefly in resignation, then burst out angrily, "Don't tell me, Jean, I don't want to know! Alright, he can do what he wants!"

I knew my father inside out, so this meant "Yes". But before I could show my joy, he interjected "Heathen! You will never get to Heaven". My mother, looking shocked, retorted "Yes, Johnny, and there'll be millions more like him".

I regard my mother as very special. She has never let her children down. When my father was alive, deeply as she loved him, she always put her children's welfare first.

There is a saying 'God couldn't give us all Jesus to love, so he gave us each a mother.' How true this saying is.

Dad calmed down and contented himself with muttering under his breath, but I had got my own way and it was GREAT!

Just then our front door bell rang. Mum went to answer the door and there was some whispering and laughter. She returned to the back room, accompanied by Gary's Gran and one of the Sunday School teachers.

'Alright John?' his Gran asked.

'Yes, not so bad', Dad replied.

Then she took up the subject. Oh no, I thought! Bad timing! But Dad didn't even blink. He was pleasant, but didn't give his opinion. The most difficult matter was yet to come. The Sunday School teacher stared hard at me, her look suggesting the importance of the question she asked:

'David, do you believe in God?'

Well, you could have knocked me down with a feather. From somewhere deep within me came a big voice, affirming His existence.

'Yes I do. Yes I do. He is all around us and he loves us'.

'Good,' she replied. 'See you on Sunday then. Oh, and I believe that you will be at the Youth Club on Thursday. It's five pence, Mrs Traynor.'

'That's fine,' Mum replied.

'Oh, and we need to know whether you will be going on the Sunday School trip to North Wales.' She winked and smiled.

'We'd better get off. Nice seeing you, Mrs Traynor, John.' With
that, they left.

I think something "clicked" with my parents that day because they
never seemed to mention religion again. I knew one thing; these people
wanted me and wanted to be my friend. They wanted to know about
me which made me feel good and besides, a Youth Club, a Sunday
School and a trip to North Wales – I was SO excited.

As my life unfolded I became even more sensitive and Senior
School proved to be a nightmare. The bullying became increasingly
brutal. As I look back to those terrible times, I realise that my parents
must have been out of their minds with worry, wondering what effect
it would have on me in later life.

My senses became heightened and they were beginning to help me
more and more to anticipate and thus avoid the bullies. I would hide
in toilets or storage rooms, empty classrooms... and as I approached
the second year in the senior school, I also became an expedient liar
– something I am not proud to admit. Lies could roll off my tongue
without my even thinking about them, just to get me out of a difficult
situation. This necessity to lie lasted only as long as I was in school, for
if it meant I would not be ridiculed, kicked or punched to the point of
not being able to breathe properly, I would do anything, say anything.
I could not escape this way of life, but, through all this torment I had
God. I also had Sunday School, Youth Club and now the Independent
Methodist Church Choir and the Sunday Service. At this time, it was
all that kept me sane.

An Evangelist, Eric Delve, came to our town and everyone, every-
where, was talking about him. One night I went along with some of
my friends from the Methodist church just to take a look. I was curious.
I didn't even know what an Evangelist was. I was deeply moved.
People sang out, they sang God's praises, they laughed and everyone
seemed happy and full of life. A long way from our Catholic church
where everyone was sombre and solemn!

At the end of the meeting, the Evangelist asked if anyone would
like to dedicate his or her life to God and I eagerly stepped forward.
It made such great changes within me. I actually felt the Holy Spirit

come alive within me – I was ignited. I was free. I can only thank Eric the evangelist, he gave me something which re-invented my life and changed the way in which I look at others.

From that moment, I came to believe that on this earthly planet, there is a place for everybody and everybody has his or her place.

Chapter 2

My First Spirit Encounter

Dad had been an undertaker for a number of years. His position as a paint sprayer and vehicle repairer had taken its toll on his health. What with the cellulose and non-ventilated spray booths, his breathing had become pretty bad. Mind you, it wasn't helped by his smoking – a roll-your-own man was my Dad.

As I look back, I believe that being an undertaker gave my father a sense of worth and self respect and apart from that, he seemed to enjoy the work. Our house had been rigged up with extra phones and bells etc. If a family had a loved one pass away during the dark hours, they would call Dad's company and automatically the call would be redirected through to our house. Dad would take the particulars and then go out, no matter what the time, and collect the body of the deceased.

If the phone rang during the night it usually woke me and as I awoke, I would know immediately whether the deceased my father was to attend was a male or female. Next morning, this "guess" was always confirmed to be accurate. It never occurred to me that it was strange that I should have this fore-knowledge.

One night, we had all retired to bed with my mother and I following our usual ritual – she kissing me and turning out the light, and I immediately turning on my bedside lamp. It was that night it happened, the appearance of the frightful apparition which I have described at the beginning of this book.

...'Whatever is the matter with you?' said my mother with an edge to her voice – alarmed by my cries but irritated about being woken. 'What's all the commotion?' my father wanted to know as he popped his head around my door.

'He's had a nightmare, that's all Johnny', Mum replied.

'He *is* a nightmare' Dad replied, making light of the situation.

As Mum left my room, she said 'I'll leave the light on while you settle down. Okay?'

'Thanks Mum', I replied gratefully.

I could hear my father hurriedly getting out of his nightwear and into his black suit. As he left the room, he popped his head around the door a second time.

'Now you get back to sleep or else you'll not get up tomorrow'. With that, he turned my light off again.

I leaned over to turn on the lamp but for some reason, didn't. I was no longer afraid of the dark.

The next morning, I awoke to hear my mother shouting from the foot of the stairs.

'Come on, David. Wake up, or you'll be late.'

'Why, what time is it?' I asked.

'Almost 8 o'clock.'

'Good grief!' My head seemed as if it were ready to burst.

I pulled myself together and went downstairs. Dad sat at the table smoking and reading the morning newspaper. The house was freezing as usual. This was due to the fact that Mum had all her life been an early riser: up at 5:30, door-knocker polished and step cleaned at 6:00, windows and back door flung open wide at 7:00 so everything was freezing cold when we came down the stairs.

'It's healthy first thing,' she'd say.

It was only when I stopped having a shower in the morning, because it was so cold, that they decided to have a gas heater installed in our bathroom.

Dad was engrossed in the sports page as usual and did not speak. I sat in front of the gas fire, turning it up onto "high". I always liked to check in the morning whether Dad had picked up a male or a female. We treated it as a game, but I was always right. This particular morning when I asked the question, my father burst out laughing. Tears rolled from his eyes.

'What's up, Dad, what have I said now?' I asked him.

'Listen to this,' he said. 'Where's your mum? Jean, come here. Listen to this. I went out to pick this chap up, he must have been in his seventies, and I gets hold of his feet and Bob got hold of him under his arms. As we lifted him, his toupé fell off! Bob dropped him with fright – he thought his head had fallen off. Bob had to sit down for ten minutes. He was still in shock when I dropped him off at home. White as a sheet he was, white as a sheet.'

Tears poured from my father's eyes. He was hysterical with laughter. I just sat there in disbelief. The penny suddenly dropped like a lead balloon. I had seen a dead man!

Chapter 3

Finding Myself

I struggled through school and believe it or not, things got a little better. I had had one or two set-backs, but this was partly due to my sensitivity to situations.

One day, towards the end of the last year at senior school, some of my class-mates engaged in a game of throwing each other down an embankment at the side of the rugby pitch. I stood watching as usual, desperate to join in, but anticipating that if I did, I should be hurt.

One of the lads in the group approached me, a boy who had never given me any "hassle" at all, someone quite insignificant in the class. This boy had somehow managed to slip through his schooldays without the slightest bit of trouble. As he approached me he smiled kindly and what he had to say made absolute sense to me.

'You'll never be accepted as an equal if you stand there being soft and just watching. That's been your trouble all the way along. You've got to join in and they'll leave you alone', and with that he got hold of my wrists, called his mate over and they seized my legs and threw me down the embankment.

I rolled over very rapidly, it felt so good. They clapped and laughed and cheered. I half expected them to jump on me, but they didn't. They just moved on to the next "victim".

Exam time had arrived and I knew that after that, my ordeal would finally come to an end. I did not present myself at many of the CSE exams. Of the ones I did turn up to sit, I copied the answers from some boys sitting around me. My technical drawing offering was a freehand copy of the work of the lad sitting in front of me, whose raised drawing board I was able to see clearly. His work was superb, mine was... well, I leave that to the reader's imagination!

I'd had enough of school.

One teacher approached me and exclaimed,

'Traynor, exam in 15 minutes.'

'Okay Sir', I said politely and then took myself off to the local park until it was all over.

Rumours flew around school of a last-day egg and flour fight, followed by a ducking in the nearby dam to clean off the evidence. Not wanting to participate in this event, I took it upon myself to leave school early. With just under three weeks to go, I walked through the metal gates of the Edmund Campion High School one happy young man. It was like something out of a Western. Everyone else was in class or exams and I just breezed through the gates and never looked back.

Nobody really cared. No representative of any Authority knocked on the door asking why I hadn't attended school. No headmaster rang mother to enquire where was I. I just disappeared into insignificance, and… it felt fantastic!

I gained a place at St. Helens College on a full-time hairdressing course. It was something I really wanted to do. I'd got the idea after seeing my cousin set up her own successful salon. How I ever came to be accepted by the College, I'll never know. They must have taken pity on me or recognised something in me that I'd overlooked.

Hairdressing was definitely me. My conversational skills grew due to regular contact with other people. Not only that, my practical skills were considered exceptional for my age and experience. At seventeen, I had a thriving mobile round, sometimes working until ten at night – even later.

I genuinely cared about my clients and, happily, I got on with each and every one of them.

I would sit and listen to them, sharing their joy and their sadness, but I wasn't *just* listening. I felt intense sympathy for them and experienced, myself, their emotions, sometimes their pain and grief, simply by standing close to them.

One day I stood putting some rollers in Doris's hair. I had known her since I was 16 and a half. I first began to roller-set her hair when I was at St. Helens College. Because she subsequently developed heart trouble, she asked my tutor if it would be possible for me to do her hair at her home.

When the teacher asked if I would mind, I told her it would be a pleasure to do it.

I had gone to Doris's home and as I roller-set her hair she began to talk about her grandson.

'You know, I wish he'd get a job,' she remarked. 'It's pure laziness, that's what it is. He'll never make anything of himself.'

She began to get upset. I put my hand on her arm and said softly, 'Doris, Mike will get a job. He's set his mind on the Police, that's why he has never committed himself to do any other work.'

Doris turned round. 'How do you know that?' she exclaimed.

'Come to think of it, how do you know his name? I've never told you anything and anyway, they live away in Somerset.'

I stood speechless. 'Oh, perhaps you did tell me Doris,' I retorted.

'Well I don't remember,' she answered firmly. 'My heart's bad, I know, but I'm all there upstairs,' she said tapping her head.

Doris never seemed the same towards me after that. I felt that she became a little less friendly, not as open with me after that conversation. Later that year she moved to Somerset where her daughter, Monica, could take care of her. She crossed over at the grand age of 79, eleven months later.

Chapter 4

Growing Up

Mum and dad had re-mortgaged their home to acquire me the lease on a hair salon just outside St. Helens town centre. My father's work-mates had thought him out of his mind putting everything he had worked for all his life on the line for me, his son.

But do you know what? He had an answer for that.

'Well, at the very least we'd have to live in a Council house if we lost ours.'

This proved to me that my parents trusted me to make this shop work and a recommended accountant, whom they had consulted, confirmed that they were making a wise investment.

As time moved on, the business began to build up and I began to put into action some of the lessons that life had taught me. The past was truly behind me, or so I thought.

Just before my twentieth birthday the shop had become so busy that we needed an apprentice and, casually, I began to mention it to my customers. One of my clients was Enid Hale. She had a daughter, Andrea, who was on the full-time hairdressing course at St. Helens College. Enid explained that she wasn't enjoying it and was, in fact, very disappointed with the whole course.

Taking advantage of the moment, I talked Enid into having her hair permed.

'Straight hair is out of fashion,' I said confidently. 'Curly's in.'

'Okay then,' she replied.

'Would you like to stay now Enid?' I enquired.

'Go on then love,' she replied. 'But you won't make it frizz will you. I don't want frizz, just soft bouncy curls'.

To this day, 20 years on, Andrea still reminds me how I turned her mum's hair into something that resembled a poodle in two hours flat!

But, I was able to glean all the information I needed about Andrea and asked Enid to get her to come to the salon for an interview.

When Andrea walked through the doors I was captivated by how pretty she was and as a result I made a slip of the tongue when I exclaimed,

'Hello *Anthea.*'

'Andrea,' she snapped back. 'Andrea. My name is Andrea'

And it was love at first sight.

I've always been ambitious and wanted to succeed and so, like many people, I went through a very odd phase in my twenties.

I've had an interest in music since I was a child. My mother can play the piano and as a youngster I'd sit and listen to her playing in our front parlour and sometimes sing along.

For some strange reason, at the age of twenty-two, I decided I could sing and even though at that young age I had a thriving business, I was willing to give it all up – believe it or not – to join the Clubland circuit.

I decided to enter a singing competition. As a preparation for this event, I talked a friend who was the owner/licensee of a pub into letting me set up my equipment in the pub's upstairs function room. Totally engrossed in my own performance, I never spared a thought for the long-suffering "regulars" below who were a captive audience.

Two weeks before the competition I learnt that my heat would be held at Stanlow, near Chester. Some of my customers had promised to come and support me at the competition. However, they were disappointed to hear that the heat to be held at St. Helens had been cancelled due to lack of support, so St. Helens contestants would have to compete in the Stanlow heat. I was not to be thwarted and hired a 52-seater coach for my supporters. One full coach and several cars turned up at a certain pub in Stanlow to discover that the landlord had forgotten to tell us that the competition had been cancelled. Disappointed, we all made our way back to my friend's pub and I sang there in front of everyone. It turned out to be a great night after all – but I realised I was no Rod Stewart and that I'd never cut a record!

However, I didn't give up that easily and, after I played a very small role in a revue for a local amateur operatic and dramatics society, my confidence grew and blossomed. It was unbelievable! I was walking around 60ft. tall and, what's more, rashly I gave up my week-day work in my salon and enrolled on a two-year drama course. I imagined myself to be the next James Bond.

Sadly, there was one thing that the drama college taught me and that was that I would never make it as a professional actor. I just couldn't hack the bravado that accompanied that particular career – and as for me being the next James Bond, well, that dream would just have to be left to *Live and Let Die...*

When the drama course ended, I went back to full-time hairdressing – a decision, I must say, I have never regretted.

As I look back on my twenties, I suppose this was a period in my life when I learnt much about myself and about life. Drama college had encouraged me to read and write, something I'd never done before. As in the play *Educating Rita,* knowledge and education freed me and for the first time in my life I felt confident. I could talk to people without shying away or feeling inferior.

So, I think my school years brought out my sensitivity, my late teens helped me to develop a sympathetic ear to my fellow man and my twenties gave me an education and the confidence not to be ashamed of who I am. Thus at the age of thirty-nine, because of my experiences and the lessons that life has taught me, (plus the precious gift of Mediumship) I find myself in a position to help others.

I had been going out with Andrea for a couple of years and we knew we were for always, there was no question of that. I got on well with her parents and Andrea with mine, which I thanked God for, because mum couldn't stand the first girlfriend I'd taken home and after she'd camped on our doorstep, she threatened her with a bucket of cold water. So, you can imagine that I was relieved.

Dad hadn't been well and one Sunday afternoon, he stood up from the table whilst he was in the middle of his Sunday lunch and blankly walked round in a circle, his eyes glazed and motionless. My mother and I both leapt up from our seats.

'Dad, dad. Are you okay?' I asked anxiously.

He seemed to come round a little, but his arms just hung by his sides. The next day mum phoned the doctor and, in turn, the specialist whom dad had seen earlier that month. He had had an X-ray which revealed two large shadows on his lungs. Mum hadn't told me – she didn't want to cause me any grief or pain. I can understand now why she did that.

That Monday afternoon, the senior specialist came out to our home. Dad sat in his chair, motionless. The specialist examined him thoroughly, explaining that it was possible that he had suffered a stroke, but the only way he could find out for sure was by admitting dad to hospital so that he could undertake further tests.

Dad was admitted to hospital. He was placed on steroids and to be honest, he returned a little to his former self. However, it was soon apparent that he had become incontinent. Each time we visited, dad began to cry and beg us to take him home. All he wanted was to go home.

At the weekend, my older brother, John, and my mother spoke with the specialist. He informed us that dad had lung cancer which had spread to his brain, where many secondary tumours had developed. The specialist held out no hope at all for dad. He offered to keep him in hospital and let him pass away there, but mum insisted that she would nurse him at home.

After seeing the specialist, mum returned home and we brought the single bed downstairs. That afternoon, we collected dad and brought him home. Lots of visitors came along but dad didn't know anybody and, day after day, his condition worsened. I sat and moved his arms and legs up and down, hour after hour to ensure his muscles wouldn't waste away.

On the Tuesday we took dad out for a ride to Southport. We had managed to borrow a wheelchair from one of my clients. We wheeled dad up and down Lord Street. Approaching the car to return home we saw that dad's trousers were wet – he had truly lost the full control of his body.

On the way back from Southport we had a flat tyre and a kind gentleman stopped and helped us change the wheel. When we got home, we changed dad and put him back in his bed.

Each day, his condition deteriorated. By the Friday we hardly recognised the man we loved.

During the early hours of Saturday morning, dad had been screaming out in agony. I came downstairs and sat behind him and held him. He just wasn't there. I knew instinctively that the hour of his death was drawing close.

Again, before Sunday morning dawned, dad screamed out with pain. I woke up and sat again behind his back holding him. I asked my mum to fetch some whisky from under the cupboard, a drink that my dad absolutely detested. Drop by drop I poured the whisky into my dad's mouth. It caused him to cough a little. I thought that if I could get him drunk, he would become insensible to pain.

The next morning, Bank Holiday Monday, 30th May 1988, I rang my brother John. I told him he had better come over as I knew that dad would die that day. John came immediately.

All that day dad was unconscious. Mum needed to keep busy, so as dad lay in the bed, John at one side of him and me at the other, mum stood by her ironing board ironing shirts and watching over us all.

At 4 o'clock that afternoon, my father crossed into the World of Spirit. As he drew his last breath I ran upstairs to my bedroom screaming,

'No, No, not my dad.'

As I did so, I threw myself on the bed. Suddenly my senses were diverted. I could tell that my dad was in the room. I looked over to the part of my bedroom near the chimney breast and there he was, in the corner, looking down at me. I turned away, looked back again and he had gone.

Chapter 5

Barry

Barry is our closest friend, here on this Earth plane, but in actual fact he is more like family. I can't find words to describe the relationship between the three of us. I don't believe there are any.

I had met Barry about five years previously at a local Operatic Society. I was rehearsing the part of Curly in *Oklahoma* and he popped in on the rehearsal and we were introduced. We had taken an instant dislike to each other, which was quite out of character for me.

Some years later I had been asked to take the lead role of Frank Butler in *Annie Get Your Gun* and Barry was in the chorus. He had been a great source of annoyance to me all through the rehearsal period. I had considered him very ill-mannered towards me and to some of the other Society members.

One evening after rehearsal he walked up to every male member in turn and asked if each of them would like to join him at the pub for a drink. Every one said "Yes". As he made his way round the hall, I thought to myself: *If he asks me I'll go along, perhaps I'll see a different side of him – maybe one that I'll like.*

They had gone to the pub every week, but I had never been invited. After asking the man standing at the side of me, Barry turned round and left the hall. My sensitivity kicked in and I felt rather emotional. I sat outside the pub for about 40 minutes, undecided whether to enter. Then, after going over the rehearsal situations and the night's events in my mind about a thousand times, I decided it wasn't worth it and began my journey home.

About half-way home, I felt an unaccountable urge to stop the car, so I pulled over and a voice in my head said, 'Call him and tell him how you are feeling.' The voice was so real I was stunned. Immediately, I stopped the car, picked up my mobile phone, pen and paper and phoned our Musical Director to ask for Barry's number.

When I rang Barry's home number, I was connected to an answering machine service, so I left a polite message and my mobile number.

Disappointed, I carried on driving and then again felt an urge to pull over, so I did. I drew into a car park, just sitting there and then my mobile phone began to ring. It was Barry. He was curious as to why I had rung. I laid my cards on the table and told the truth. Seemingly, Barry hadn't wanted to get involved with me – I wasn't his type of person, I was too "loud" for him. Barry also admitted that making friends wasn't his strongest attribute. We agreed that we would make the effort just for the sake of the production.

During the week leading up to the show and throughout the show's run Barry and I really got to know one another. I felt as if I had known him all my life. He was one of the most sincere people I had ever met. He had battled with diabetes and its pernicious effects on his life for fifteen years.

During the months after the show we became good friends and then soul mates. Twelve months down the line, my wife and I, not having any children or dependents, asked Barry to come and live with us – our house is rather large for two. At first he was a little unsure, being single for so long and living alone. Eventually, he decided to move in and none of us have ever looked back.

Rather strangely, a few months later, Barry discovered he could draw people who had crossed over to the World of Spirit.

Chapter 6

Introductions

It was boom time in Britain for the housing market and Andrea and I had decided that we would like to move to an old house. We had lived in new houses all of our married life. One night, Andrea was searching the Internet to see what properties were available in the areas surrounding our present home when she discovered, to her delight, a house we had liked eighteen months previously that had come on to the market again. The very next day we rang for an appointment to view. We loved it so much we engaged an estate agent to sell our house immediately. It sold in just 24 hours for the full asking price.

By this time, lots of people were after the old house. It was a rat race, but after much frustration I wrote directly to the owners of the house pleading with them to let us have it. A few days later, the estate agent rang and told us the house was ours. We were overjoyed.

The house has a beautiful homely feel to it and lots of character. We felt at home right from the word "go". After moving in, we discovered shadows moving across the wall. These shadows took the shape of people. Neither Andrea nor I have ever felt disturbed or concerned by this, we just laugh and we called them our friends.

It was after buying this house that my spiritual journey seemed to take a large step forward. I decided to join the local amateur operatic society and remember, that's where I met Barry, not my favourite person at that time.

Just a few weeks before we moved into the house we purchased another shop, which was our third. All the upheaval was very stressful for me. One day, Jayne, our manageress, rang up from our main branch to speak to me. She asked if I would like a Tarot card reading. She explained that Sarah, one of the hairdressers, had invited a psychic to read the cards at her home. The readings were £20 each, but Sarah needed five people and she had only four.

'Go on then, I'll give it a go,' I said apprehensively.

I knew nothing about Tarot reading and fortune telling. Not only had I never had my own cards read, but I didn't even know anyone who had had theirs read either. What I *did* know, though, was that if my mother found out what I had agreed to do, she would have strongly disapproved.

Later that day one of the girls at the salon let the cat out of the bag. Mum waited in the staff room quietly.

'You are not going to have your Tarot cards read, are you?' she said.

'Yes I am. Why mum?' I replied.

'It's a load of rubbish, David. You are not supposed to believe in such tomfoolery and furthermore, it's bad luck. You are flying in God's face. There is no one, no one anywhere who can tell you what the future holds. How much is it then? A bloody fortune I bet.'

'Mum. Will you leave me alone,' I said. 'I'm not a child', and with that I left.

That afternoon, I'd heard story after story of clients who'd had bad experiences after using ouija boards and staff who had had Tarot card readings which had proved remarkably accurate. Someone knew someone who had been "possessed".

Still, I am my mother's son, that's for sure, and when I say I'm going to do something, I do it. I wasn't going to be put off and that night at seven o'clock I knocked on Sarah's door.

I was invited in. Four girls sat sipping wine and Sarah's little boy was playing with his toy cars on the carpet.

'Do you want a drink David?' Sarah asked.

'No, I'm fine Sarah, I left a drink at the pub,' I replied. 'Where is she then, the Tarot card reader?'

'The "she" is a "he",' Sarah said laughing. 'He just needs fifteen minutes to settle in.'

'Whose going first?' Jayne asked.

'May I Jayne? I've left my mother and Andrea at the pub.' I had said I would join the Tarot session but had forgotten that I'd made arrangements to have dinner at the local pub with my mum and wife. This, I believe, had added to mum's annoyance over the situation.

A tall, thin man with curly hair, dressed like a hippie, appeared at Sarah's living room door. He smiled and immediately left the room. Sarah looked at me and urged, 'Go on then, you go first.'

'Let us know what he says,' Jayne called.

Nervously I entered the dining room and sat down.

'Make yourself at home,' said the man, then paused and staring at me asked inquisitively, 'why have you come here?'

'For a laugh,' I replied.

'Oh well, I hope I make you laugh then.'

He boxed his Tarot deck with all the professionalism of a croupier in a casino. Then he laid the cards face up on the table in the shape of a cross.

'You are a medium,' he said.

'No,' I stated. 'I'm a 36-inch waist. I was a 32-inch but I've put on weight,'. I genuinely thought he was talking about my size for some unknown reason.

'I don't mean your size,' he laughed. 'You communicate with the After World. You see, you have a lot of energy. Your aura is a deep purple, this means that you are a very spiritual person. This also shows in your cards. Here and here.'

He indicated several cards.

'I feel you have been mediumistic since you were a child. Does the name Maria mean anything to you?'

'Yes,' I replied flabbergasted. 'I do understand. She was...'

'Don't tell me,' he interjected. 'I'll tell *you*, okay? That's what I'm here for. I want to emphasize a friendship link with Maria. She was your friend, but there was something different about this friendship. However, I will say no more about this,' he said dramatically.

'Okay,' I said but my knees were beginning to tremble. I was desperately trying to hide my fear.

'Now, I see "abroad" for you. I want to go to Italy for ten days,' he added. 'Do you understand?' he asked.

'No chance! I'm going nowhere on a plane,' I retorted and I meant it. The 9/11 tragedy in America a short while before had taken away a small piece of my freedom. I'd resigned myself to holidaying in English resorts.

'You will go to Italy my friend,' he insisted. 'Now, I have the impression of moving house and this is a good move. A good move for you and your wife and it will change your life for ever.'

'We have considered moving,' I said, 'in the near future'.

'Now, who is Andrea?' he asked.

'My wife,' I replied.

'Is she petite and blonde?'

'Yes she is,' I replied, wondering what he would say next.

'She is a good girl. A bit headstrong, but she will be there for you throughout all your changes.'

'What changes?' I asked.

'Life's changes,' he replied. 'You are on a spiritual journey. You have been given the gift of mediumship and you must use it for the good of all, but there are going to be big changes. You will begin to see situations much more clearly than you did before. Your emotions will be heightened and you will share the joy and pain of the people who need your help.'

Very profound, I thought to myself, but I was not convinced of what he said.

'Eventually you will stand up and demonstrate your mediumship in front of audiences here and in America. There will be books about you and your life. Remember what I've said friend.'

I couldn't help thinking I'd wasted my money but at the same time I didn't understand how he could know so much about me. Then, out of the blue he said, 'Your dad's here – Johnny. He's with you all the time. He's got glasses and white wavy hair.'

'Oh my goodness,' I exclaimed.

'He says you're a good lad and you're going to be a great success here on Earth.'

'Thank you,' I said emotionally.

'Now go in peace friend,' he said.

As I stood up to leave he smiled and said 'That's £20 please.'

I handed him the money and left.

'What did he say? What did he say, go on tell us?' Jayne asked eagerly.

Sarah asked, 'Is he any good David?'

'He's excellent! Amazing! Brilliant! 'He told me things that no one could possibly know, except me. I'll tell you all about it at work on Wednesday, but I must go, my mum and Andrea will be wondering where I've got to.'

I paused in the doorway and announced, 'I can do what he does.'

Jayne laughed and replied,' You'll have to "do" me then. Tell me if I'm gonna get myself a fella.'

Heading back to the pub my mind was alive with what the Tarot reader had said. As I approached the building, I noticed my mum and Andrea shivering in the doorway.

'Where've you been?' mum said annoyed.

'You've been ages,' Andrea announced.

I just knew it was going to be one of those long journeys home!

On the following Friday the salon was busy as usual. I'd been in and out of the staff room all that morning talking about my Tarot reading. My colleagues were intrigued. I prudently omitted some of the information that had been imparted to me. I wanted a little more proof of my apparent abilities before announcing their existence.

Six o'clock that evening saw the arrival of my friend Elaine for her regular weekly blow-dry. I always know when Elaine wants me to tell her something because she just looks at me and laughs and doesn't speak, which I might add is a little unusual for the lass – not to speak that is.

'Well?' she began, as she sat before the mirror.

'It was brilliant,' I said. 'But he told me something which is very private and I feel a bit uneasy about it.'

'Can I make a suggestion?' Elaine said. Her suggestions usually make a lot of sense to me.

'Go on,' I prompted.

'I've got a friend called Jane who also reads Tarot cards. If you consult her and she says the same as the Tarot man said at Sarah's, then you'll know there's something in it.'

'Elaine, you're a gem,' I said smiling.

'At least it will put your mind at rest, David. Here's her phone number.'

After Elaine left, I telephoned Jane to book an appointment. Conveniently, she'd had a cancellation for the next day at 5–30.

It was seven o'clock and another Friday over with! A shattered staff stood drinking tea and coffee in the staff room.

'I've booked an appointment to see another psychic tomorrow, ' I announced.

'Not another!' one of the girls remarked.

'I just need to know the answers to some questions. I can't tell you what they are yet. I'm not mad. I know I sound like a Tarot junkie but I have my reasons.'

Mum had entered the back door and caught the tail end of the conversation.

'Bloody hell! You're not still going on about that rubbish are you?'

'He's off to another one tomorrow Jean,' one of the girls offered.

'Again!' she exclaimed. 'I can see where you'll be ending up lad – in Rainhill.' Rainhill had been a psychiatric hospital for years until it was demolished and an estate of four- and five-bedroom luxury houses now stand on its site.

'Well mum, if I end up in Rainhill I'll have done very well for myself,' I joked.

Mum went into story-telling mode. 'When I was a girl there was a woman who read tea leaves and told fortunes. We called her "Black Lucy". If you had a problem you went to her – paid half a crown and she'd give you the answers. She was always right, Black Lucy was. She knew everything about everything.'

Something suddenly dawned on me. How did my mother know all this about Black Lucy? Had she in her youth been a "fallen angel" too?

'Well. I'd better get off then,' I said.

'More money than sense you have,' she chipped in as I closed the shop door.

Very anxiously at 5–30 on Saturday, I stood before the door of a rather large house. Nervously I rang the doorbell. The door opened to reveal a tall, attractive lady casually dressed in jumper and jeans.

'Hello, are you David?' she asked kindly.

I replied in the affirmative.

'Take a seat in here.' She pushed the door open. 'I won't be a moment.

As I entered the room a sense of calm came over me which was very welcome after the busy day I'd had. I sat down in a comfortable, high-backed chair, and began to study my surroundings.

Jane entered the room, 'Would you like a glass of water?' she asked.

'No thanks. I'm fine.'

She went away, presumably to attend to several barking dogs. I returned to my visual examination of the room. Jane returned and sat down in the chair opposite me.

'Have you ever been for a reading before David?' she asked.

'Yes, I have,' I replied.

'Well, you'll know what happens then,' she commented. 'Now. I'll just close my eyes and see what I get… . I want to say your dad's in Spirit,' she said. 'He's very much like you David – your build and facial features. Do you understand?'

'Yes, Jane,' I replied.

'And your mum's mum is here too, by the name of Maggie. A very nice lady, quite plump – always washed her hands when she was here on the Earth plane.'

'That's true Jane. My grandmother was actually washing her hands at the time when she died.'

'It is this lady from whom you've inherited your Gift.'

My knees began to tremble again.

'Stop trembling. You're a Psychic Medium. There's nothing wrong with that. Besides, I've never known a hairdresser not to have that Gift – in different degrees of course.'

How does she know I'm a hairdresser? I thought to myself.

'Because hairdressers are in close proximity to their clients. Do you know when you're cutting their hair, you're in your customer's space,' she explained.

'And that's how you've become sensitive to people because your aura blends with theirs.'

This didn't make much sense to me at all. I was already reeling from the shock of learning that she knew I was a hairdresser, when she said, 'Barry. You've met a guy called Barry whom you don't really like; he annoys you.'

'Yes Jane, he does,' I replied.

'Well he's going to become your closest friend and move into your home with you and your wife.'

This sounded far fetched to me, and highly unlikely.

'There's a diabetic connection in relation to Barry.'

'Yes, there is Jane.'

'Now. You're a very strong medium yourself, David. The spirits want you to work for them here on the Earth plane. I'm being told that you'll be demonstrating before audiences here and in America. There will be books written about you, TV and radio interviews. It's all going to change your life drastically.'

By this time my knees had stopped knocking and I was beginning to come to terms with what Jane had said. She asked me to choose some Tarot cards from her pack. When I had done so Jane interpreted them for me. She gave me much information about my business, holidays, finance, family matters and personal relationships – all of it, sooner or later, proving to be accurate.

'Now, David,' she said. 'Have you ever communicated with people in the Spirit World?'

'No Jane, I haven't.' I could feel my knees beginning to shake again.

'Well, with your Gift you should. Shall I show you what to do?'

'Oh no, Jane. I'm terrified of that sort of stuff.'

'You're a very gifted young man,' she said. 'The energy's immense around you and you will be a brilliant medium.'

'Well, we'll see Jane,' I said dismissively.

I think Jane was aware that she would be unable to persuade me to take up her offer. After a moment, she smiled and said, 'Well, I hope I've been of help to you and I hope I've answered some of your questions. I know you'll be seeing me again very soon, David.'

I looked at Jane and replied, 'I know you will Jane, but I need to get my head around what you've said first.'

I thanked her and left. I had never met anyone as serene as Jane. Her ability amazed me.

The following Wednesday I was working in my third salon. It was unusually "slack" that day. Cheryl, one of my colleagues, announced she had gone out shopping the day before and bought some Tarot cards. Without even thinking, I exclaimed, 'I can read those.'

'Well, I've got them with me,' Cheryl said, hurrying to fetch them. 'I'll show you.'

She exited through the staff room door. A customer, Debbie, was having her hair coloured. She had never been in the salon before. She seemed friendly and quite "chatty".

'I'd love to have a Tarot reading,' Debbie said out loud. 'I've never had one before, but I've always said I would.'

Cheryl returned holding some large cards.

'These must be learner's cards,' I joked, taking them from her.

'Why?' Jane said.

'Because of the size of the syllables on the cards,' I told her.

'When could you read for me?' Debbie asked.

'Now. While your colour's processing,' I offered.

'Okay,' she said.

'You'll need to go into the back room,' Jayne informed her.

'I took a towel from the towel-holder and put it around my head like a wimple.

'What's that for?' Jayne said.

'Just to get me in the mood. They call me Septic Peg, the gypsy,' I joked.

'Can you really do this?' Jayne asked seriously.

'YES,' I replied, making my way into the back room.

'Sit here Debbie.' I began to copy what I had seen done in the readings I had had. Letting Debbie shuffle the cards I instructed her to pick eight cards randomly from the pack and I laid the chosen cards on the work surface in the shape of a cross. I looked at the pictures and told Debbie what came into my head.

After a while, the realisation came to me that she was nodding agreement when I described events which had happened to her. This made me very nervous. I decided to tell her silly things concerning situations which could not possibility be real. The strange – and to me, totally shocking – thing was, she continued to nod agreement, confirming that what I said was meaningful to her.

As time went on, the information I imparted became less general and more specific, so much so that I could tell she was becoming uncomfortable and so was I.

I decided to call it a day. Debbie was called over to the backwash to have the chemicals rinsed from her hair. I was totally shocked by the whole situation, a million and one questions running through my head.

The first question I sought an answer to was, 'where had the information come from?' Secondly, 'was I mind-reading unknowingly?'

I decided to try reading the cards again. Sue and Jayne volunteered themselves. After I'd finished, the verdict was unanimous. 'You've gotta Gift, David,' Sue said in a psuedo-American accent.

I needed to assimilate all that had happened. Perhaps many people would be delighted to discover they have such a gift. I was terrified.

I decided that enough was enough. That afternoon found me trembling and stammering at Jane's door.

'Hello David,' she said. 'I see you've read the Tarot cards then.'

I looked at her in total disbelief. 'Yes, I'm going out of my mind Jane. What's going to happen to me next?' I asked.

'You'd better come in and take a seat in my office.'

Jane sat opposite me in the high green chair. 'You got everything right, didn't you David?'

'Yes I did, but it was scary,' I said.

'Well I did say I'd see you soon, didn't I, David? Now, you need to know about your particular Gift. How to use it properly. Does it have any limitations? Let me see now... you've heard of the chakras? They are the seven energy points in our body.'

'No, I haven't. I don't know what you're talking about,' I said.

'Have you ever meditated?' Jane wanted to know.

'No, never,' I replied.

'Wow! Then you *have* got a Gift. I knew you had when I first met you – your energy is so strong. I thought you might have helped it along a little.' She looked thoughtful. 'And you've never contacted anyone in the world of Spirits?' she asked.

'Never,' I replied.

'Look. I'll take you through a simple exercise. Don't be nervous. Relax. Close your eyes. Imagine beautiful golden roots coming out of the ends of your toes and burrowing deep into the ground. If you can't see those roots in your mind's eye, just tell yourself that they are there. Now, as you've got your roots into the ground, I want you to imagine a beautiful, white light and I want you to draw the white light up through the roots, through your feet, up through your knees, through to your waist, up through your body and your neck, through your head and out of the crown of your head. Now try that again.'

Her voice was hypnotic. I became so relaxed, I almost felt I was floating.

'I would like you to imagine the house where you lived as a child. Pretend you're a silent visitor, like a ghost. Look at the front door. Can you see it in your mind's eye?' she asked.

'Yes,' I replied, quietly.

'Walk through the door and over to the bottom of the staircase. Now, I want you, in your head, to ask for someone to meet you at the top of the staircase.'

'I'm a bit scared, Jane,' I said.

'Don't be. Nothing can harm you. I'm here, David,' she reassured.

'Okay, I'll trust you,' I said.

I started to walk up the staircase in my imagination, step by step.

'Are you at the top?'

'Yes'

'Who's joined you David. Tell me.'

'No-one Jane,' I replied. The words hadn't left my mouth when the back bedroom door opened and my Gran, who had passed away when I was a baby, walked through it. I recognised her from some of my mother's old photographs.

'My Gran has joined me, Jane,' I said.

'Good, say hello to her then.'

'Hello, Gran,' I said out loud.

She began to smile. 'Hello, David love,' she replied, but what was strange was that her reply was not in spoken words but in my thoughts, which seemed to be impressed upon me. Each individual word that came into my head seemed to be weighted, which separated them from my own thoughts.

'Is it really you, Gran?' I said.

'Yes, love,' she replied.

I couldn't change my inner focus. She was SO real.

'Time to leave her now,' Jane said. 'Say goodbye to her.'

''Bye, Gran,' I said.

'Goodbye, love, see you again.' She turned around and walked back into the bedroom, closing the door behind her.

'Now walk back down the stairs,' Jane said softly. 'Out through the door and open your eyes. Now… how do you feel?' Jane asked.

'Very, very nervous,' I answered. 'Not scared – that's gone. Was I really speaking to my Gran?' I asked.

'You were. Who's Maggie?' Jane asked confidently.

'That's her, that's my Gran,' I replied.

'Then yes, you were. That simple exercise enables you to contact your loved ones on the other side,' Jane explained. 'If you do the same exercise but ask your guides to join you, you should be able to meet them too. That may take a little longer so be patient if you do decide to do that. Always remember to put down your roots into the ground before you start and if you get stuck, give me a call.'

'Forgive my ignorance Jane, is that what mediums do – meditate and then contact people who have died?'

'Yes. Look… take a drive to Chorley Spiritualist Church on

Thursday evenings and you'll see a medium in action. It's not scary, so don't worry and they have a Circle after.'

'What's that?' I asked inquisitively.

'A Circle? It's where young mediums like yourself develop. You'll be known as a "fledgeling". It will dispel all your fears and answer a lot of questions.'

'Okay Jane, I will go to Chorley on Thursday and I'll call you and let you know how I got on, if that's alright.'

'Do, I'll look forward to it,' Jane replied.

'Thanks, Jane. Thanks for everything.'

'No problem,' was her comment.

As we got to her front door she stopped and looked intently at me. 'You know David, you are going to be a very famous medium. There will be books written about you, radio and TV interviews. I want you to remember what I have said.'

I looked at her, stunned by what I heard. In a somewhat mysterious voice, Jane reiterated, 'Remember, David.'

I thanked her, wished her good night and left.

Chapter 7

A Fledgeling Medium

It was proving to be difficult finding someone to accompany me to the Spiritualist Church that week. I made a number of phone calls, and strangely, all the people whom I asked were suddenly very busy on the night of the Spiritualist Church service. Finally, there was only Barry's name left on the list. At that time, I had not known him very long, and still considered some of his ways rather strange. However, he *did* owe me a couple of favours. I had arranged one or two "blind dates" for him which – although they had not led to long-term romantic relationships – had resulted in his making some good friends.

Surprisingly, Barry agreed to come along. He seemed unperturbed by the nature of the proposed venue, in fact he looked rather interested. He agreed to pick me up since he said he knew Chorley like the back of his hand – it seemed a good suggestion.

We arrived at the church after the service had started. We had got lost on the way and had to ask several passers-by before we found someone who knew the whereabouts of the church. The congregation was singing a hymn as Barry and I sneaked in and stood at the back. The room was full to over-flowing.

When the hymn was over everyone sat down and a lady of smart appearance stood up. She had grey-blond hair and looked to be in her early seventies. Her face was heavily made up. She spoke with a Liverpool accent and asked us all to bow our heads in prayer. Then she invited us to recite the Lord's Prayer together. Next she began to speak about her experiences as a medium, which I found to be very interesting. As I looked at Barry out of the corner of my eye I saw that he was yawning. Then the lady announced that she would be doing a demonstration of clairvoyance. She pointed to a lady sitting on the front row of the congregation and asked for her permission to talk to her. This lady nodded and smiled.

'A gentleman called Arthur has joined me from the World of Spirit,' she announced. 'I believe he's your husband, my love.'

'Yes,' the lady replied.

'He crossed at the age of 59. Can you understand my love?'

'Yes, he did,' the lady replied.

'He had lung cancer and he died in Chorley Hospital.'

'Yes, he did', the lady replied. She was becoming emotional and there was a quiver in her voice.

'He says he loves you. Who is Carol?' the medium asked, suddenly.

'I'm Carol'', the lady replied wiping away her tears with a tissue.

'He loves you lots, Carol, and he wants to send his love to the girls. Will you tell the girls, Carol?'

'Yes, yes I will,' Carol replied, eagerly.

'God bless you, my dear.'

Carol looked overwhelmed. I later discovered that it had been the first anniversary of her husband's death a couple of weeks before and she'd hoped for some communication from him.

I looked out of the corner of my eye again at Barry. He seemed to be asleep. I immediately felt anxious – there was a distinct possibility that he could fall over.

'I want to come to you, sir. Yes you, standing up at the back, and you love. Are you still with us?' the medium bellowed.

I nudged Barry. He opened his eyes. He *had* been fast asleep and was startled by his sudden awakening.

'Am I boring you, lad?' she joked.

Everyone in the congregation began to laugh out loud. I could feel myself getting hotter and hotter. My cheeks felt as if they were on fire.

'Now. Can I speak to you both,' she said, raising her voice so we could hear her at the back.

'Yes, yes,' we replied in unison.

'Now, the Spirits are telling me they want you to work for them. Yes, you sir,' she pointed to me. 'You are a medium and you sir,' –

here she indicated Barry – 'You are a Psychic Artist and you will both be up here taking your own services before long. I am being told that your lives have been difficult, but that these difficulties have taught both of you lessons which will help you along the way. I feel that your friendship has not been easy.'

'No, no it hasn't', I said.

'Well it will get easier. Trust me,' the medium said. 'You must both find a Development Circle. Now one of you is artistic.'

'That's me,' I replied.

'The other one likes computers. I'm computer illiterate,' she joked.

'I do,' Barry confirmed, 'I like computers.'

'You're a good team. The Spirits are telling me to tell you to get on with it. So I'll leave you with that thought and I will say good night and God bless to you both.'

'Thanks. Thanks a lot,' I said. Barry echoed what I had said.

After the service tea and coffee were served. Everyone seemed friendly. Barry and I stood apart sipping our drinks.

'Do you know, Barry, I think I'll ask that medium if she can recommend a Circle we could attend?'

Barry thought this a good idea. As we approached together, we were both aware that she knew what we were going to ask, but we said it anyway.

'Is there a good Circle we could join?' we asked.

'Yes. Moor Lane in Preston'. She fumbled in her handbag, saying, 'I've got a number here somewhere. The man you need to speak to is Jim Roe. He's the head medium, you'll be okay with Jim – he's very experienced and he's turned out some good mediums in his time.'

She handed me Jim's number. I thanked her.

'Can you tell us our guide's names please?' Barry asked.

'Yours,' she said pointing to Barry, 'is an Indian, but I can't quite pick up his name. Yours,' pointing to me, 'is a Greek man called "Conquistry". He will work with you.' I must admit I never saw

Conquistry. Maybe he did exist, but didn't like the look of me – his intended medium. It wasn't long after that that Jason made himself known to me and has worked with me ever since.

'Thanks,' I said.

'Are you staying for the Circle?' she asked.

'Yes,' said Barry eagerly.

Well, well! Where did that bout of enthusiasm come from? I thought to myself. Aloud I said,

'Yes, we will stay for the Circle.'

'Good. It's psychometry tonight, which is a good exercise when you are starting out.' She smiled and left us.

'I'll be alright for the lottery now, Barry,' I joked. 'I'll ask "Conquistry" for the lucky numbers.'

Barry managed to smile.

A circle of chairs had been put out in the centre of the hall. People began making their way over to them and sitting down, so we followed. A smart-looking lady with dark curly hair began by saying, 'Shush everybody, please.' Her accent was "really Northern".

'Shush, please,' she repeated loudly. 'Now, its Psychometry tonight. Is there anyone who has not done Psychometry before? Please raise your hands.'

Five of us did so.

'Well, what I would like you to do is place a piece of jewellery or one of your personal belongings on the tray that is going to be passed around the circle.'

One or two people appeared doubtful, others looked worried.

'Right, I'm off to a car boot sale,' she joked.

Everyone burst into laughter. The ice was broken.

'Now, I want each of you to go over to the tray and pick up an item belonging to someone else. Find out who it belongs to, hold it in your right hand and tell them everything that comes into your mind. Can you all do that?'

Several people didn't look enthusiastic at all. I was raring to go. I walked over to the tray and picked up a lady's silver watch with a blue face. When I held it up, a lady beckoned to me.

'Hello,' I said. 'How are you?'

'Okay love.' Her accent was Irish.

The information flowed from me. I talked to the lady about her disabled son. I told her his name, David. I knew her job – she was a care assistant in a nursing home. Then a man came into my mind's eye. He told me his name, again by emphasising strongly... THOMAS.'

'That's my Dad,' she said loudly. 'You've contacted my Dad.'

'Belfast,' I said.

'That's where all our family come from. Oh bless you son, bless you.' I was greatly affected by her obvious joy. I thanked her for listening and sat down, surprised at my own overwhelming emotion.

I felt pleased with myself. Although I knew myself to be a successful businessman and enjoyed my work greatly, it had never given me the degree of satisfaction I had just experienced.

During the car journey home, Barry and I could hardly get out our words to each other fast enough. We were both elated, exhilarated. We sat in the car outside my house still talking nineteen to the dozen. Barry suddenly pulled off his wrist watch.

'Go on then', he said, 'see what you can get from *my* watch.'

Hesitantly and somewhat nervously, I took the watch. After a slight pause I began to list the names of his family members, here and in the After Life. I described to him situations about which it would normally be impossible for a third party to have any knowledge.

At 11–30 I was still rattling off all kinds of information. Barry verified that it was all correct. Suddenly, I broke off, noticing Barry's weariness and realising how late it was.

'You're shattered, Barry. Go home to bed, we'll talk tomorrow.'

'Okay. It's been great hasn't it? Same again next week?' he smiled.

'Same again next week,' I agreed.

The next day I gave Jim Roe a call and arranged to meet him that afternoon at 2 o'clock. As I pulled up in my car outside the Moor Lane Spiritualist Church in Preston, I couldn't help wondering what Jim would have to say.

It was with some trepidation that I walked in through a very large oak door. Inside, the church seemed no different from any other church I had been in. At the front, there was a rostrum and in the centre was a beautiful lectern. Around the altar were draped heavy, purple velvet curtains. On the proscenium were the words "All we love, live". *Very apt,* I thought.

Pausing at the back of the church, I looked towards the front. My eye travelled along a wide aisle with pews to either side.

'Come in,' a voice said from a corner behind me. I turned to face a tall man, smiling and offering his hand.

'I'm Jim Roe – you're David?'

'Yes I am. Pleased to meet you,' I replied.

'Have a seat, David. Would you like some tea or coffee?' he offered.

'No thanks.'

'Well in that case, what can I do for you?' he asked.

'Well I think I've got a Gift, Jim, and it's been suggested that you might help me.' I began to explain about the psychic readings I had had and my own experience of reading the Tarot cards in the salon. I told him about the psychometry and how all the details were correct.

'I think it is possible you are a medium, David, and with the clarity of your evidence during your own attempts at reading, I would say you've been a medium since you were a child. It is possible that you have been developing without being aware of it. As a hairdresser, you work in close proximity to your clients, that is, you enter their personal space and, because you are a sensitive young man, your awareness of them and how they are feeling would manifest without you realising. Each level of your sensitivity would be exercised until your aware-ness was unbelievably heightened.'

What Jim was saying made complete sense to me. I had always been sensitive to my customers' needs, aside from hairdressing, even when their need was simply for advice – in short, I had always cared.

Jim invited me to join his Development Circle which was held in the church every Friday. He explained that he would thus be able to observe my Gift to discover exactly what it entailed and how it manifested itself.

He said he sensed that I was a clairvoyant, which means 'clear sighted.' He also thought there was a possibility that I might be clairsentient, which means I can sense and feel what is going on around me. Excited by the whole project, I took Jim up on his offer and agreed to attend the following Friday.

I had read a book about the life of a medium which had given me the impression that a Development Circle consisted of five people. This idea was dispelled when I turned up on the Friday. People of all different ages took their places within the Circle of pre-set seats. There were fifteen in total that night, all seeming really nice. Jim stood at the helm.

'Ladies and gentlemen I would like to introduce David Traynor to our Circle,' he announced. 'David believes he has a Gift – the Gift of mediumship and I am sure he is right. Tonight, using our own gifts of communication with the Spirit world, we are going to try to help him to confirm the existence of this gift and its nature. Will you please settle down, so we may begin with a prayer?'

Jim began to pray. In his opening prayer he asked for peace in the world and help for people on beds of sickness and then he thanked the Great Spirit for all the good in the world. After hearing such a lovely prayer, I knew I was in the presence of a truly spiritual man.

Jim then led us through a guided meditation, which was complemented by subtle background music. In the relaxed atmosphere, my imagination conjured up rich and varied imagery.

When Jim brought us back to our conscious state, he asked if anyone had a message from the World of Spirit and if they had, would they relay it to the individual for whom it was meant.

In turn, people gave each other messages from the other side. A gentleman joined me from the other side and requested me to pass a message to a lady sitting to my right on the far side of the circle. When my turn came to speak, I asked her if she was happy to receive messages. She said she was.

Through my lips, the conversation flowed. The gentleman gave his name and her name. He told her all about her childhood and her life at that time, adding that she would be entering on a new business venture. All the information was received by the lady and affirmed to be correct. When the communication had ceased, Jim smiled his approval.

At last, the Circle closed and the participants began to prepare to leave the Church. I wondered what Jim would say to me about the demonstration of communication with the Spirit world. He said he had no hesitation in recommending that I should develop my Gift further. He added that he believed I would become a well-known medium – 'An overnight phenomenon,' he remarked.

It had been an eventful six months since I discovered my capabilities as a medium. I'd already taken part in a demonstration at Moor Lane Church, with four other "fledgelings", and it had been very successful. Also I had gained my first booking as a professional spirit medium.

On the night of this booking, I walked into Moor Lane Church consumed with nerves, fearful of letting down my audience and failing to do justice to my gift.

At that stage, I had been demonstrating mediumship for the best part of a year. Most of my events are local – at St. Helens, Liverpool, Preston, Blackpool and not forgetting Wigan. The response has been phenomenal. Crowds of people come along in the hope that their loved ones will give them a message and my aim is to try to give out as many messages as I can during the demonstration.

I absolutely love my work as a spirit medium. I feel I'm helping people to come to terms with the natural progression of life – which is death, one of life's greatest lies. For as I know now, life goes on – death is not final.

Chapter 8

Years Later

I was woken from my nap by Andrea. 'Tea's on the table, love.'

'Coming,' I replied. I felt shattered. It had been a busy day at the salon. Mondays are traditionally not very busy at the hairdressers, but today had been packed. Walking into the kitchen, Andrea commented, 'Just something light, love, a Caesar salad and a glass of water.' She had a big smile on her face.

'Thanks,' I replied.

'You carry on love, our steak's not quite done enough.'

I could have killed for a 10oz. sirloin with onion rings and fries. Andrea is a great cook, always has been. Cookery and Domestic Science were her number one subjects at school, although she wouldn't have wanted to be a professional cook.

'Where's Barry?' I asked.

'Meditating, love, upstairs. I'd better give him a shout, his tea's nearly ready.'

'Barry, tea's in five minutes!' Andrea yelled from the bottom of the stairs.

'Thanks Andrea,' a distant voice replied.

Shortly afterwards, a rather jaded looking Barry entered the kitchen.

'Better take a blood test,' he muttered.

'You low?' I queried.

'Feels a bit suspect,' he replied weakly. As he tested, Andrea filled our plates with a lovely tea. She poured two glasses of red wine and recorked the bottle.

'What time's your sitting then?' Barry asked.

'7 o'clock,' I replied.

'3.2' he interjected. 'Well, looks like it's time for food. I'll jab half way through dinner. I should be okay then,' he confirmed.

I was seeing two people that night, Bev and her father. I didn't know his name and I only knew his daughter's name because that was what she had called herself when she had booked to see me.

I had met Bev and her father at one of my demonstrations in Preston, Lancashire. It had been a great night. There had been several strong contacts made and one particular contact had stood out in my mind. It was with a Spirit gentleman called Bill Roberts.

Bill had actually woken me during the early hours of Tuesday, 25th May. A very large man, he stood there calling, 'David, David.'

I became conscious and I could see and hear him clearly as he spoke to me.

'Hi, who are you?' I said in my head voice. For those of you who are wondering, my "head voice" is that voice I hear when I'm talking within myself, when I am communicating with those in the Spirit World. It is similar to the sensation you may be feeling now as you read this book quietly to yourself.

'I'm Bill Roberts,' he replied. 'My daughter's coming over to your demonstration tonight and I want to contact her. I'm desperate.'

And to be honest, he sounded it.

I explained to him that it was 3–45 in the morning, Earth plane time and I was in bed asleep.

'I'm so sorry,' he replied.

I told him that if he came back later I would gladly mediate for him. With that, he thanked me and left. It is necessary to explain that time does not exist in the Spirit World so there is no need for watches, whereas here in our physical world, our planet turns giving us night and day.

That night he came through to his daughter who sat waiting pensively in the audience. Through me, he was able to verify himself by his full name and some personal details such as where and how he had crossed over. He also gave other family members' names, including his daughter's.

The message had been a poignant one. After the demonstration, his daughter walked up to me, thanked me and told me that what I had said was what she had needed to hear, and giving me a huge hug, she left the hall.

As I sat sipping my coffee, my thoughts turned to Bev and her father. I had gone over to her during my demonstration, but she had not been able to take any of the information at all that I was imparting. I had felt a natural barrier around her for some reason.

Incidentally, the lady sitting two seats away from Bev took all the evidence and we had established an excellent communication with her mum, Maureen, a retired school teacher from Durham.

Bev approached me and said, 'Hi'.

'Hello there,' I replied. She seemed alone at first and then I realised that her father was standing behind her. I felt he was a little embarrassed.

'Can I ask you something please, David?' she asked politely.

'Fire away,' I replied.

At this point, her father slowly began to make his way forward.

'I just wondered why you are able to communicate so well for everyone else and you came over to me and it didn't happen. We've come along here tonight desperate to hear from someone.'

I could sense the disappointment in her voice and, in addition, as her dad stepped closer to me, I could feel his sadness deep within my heart. One of the downsides to being a medium is that you can't get round to everyone in a demonstration situation. Sometimes, you just don't connect. I have been very successful so far, but there have been people with whom it has been impossible to communicate. However, my many successes far outweigh the number of failures.

'Now, maybe your mum couldn't be here tonight,' I replied.

'How did you know it was my mum?' she questioned.

'Because I am a medium and my guide, Jason, has informed me

that your mum has not been long in the World of Spirit, so she isn't yet evolved enough to communicate, but he says she is doing fine.'

Bev and her dad looked astonished.

'Do you do private sittings? You know, on a one-to-one basis? Well, my dad would need to come along too.'

'Only for the needy,' I stressed. Jason told me that her father was finding it difficult to cope. In my experience, and not meaning to sound sexist, widows always seem to cope better than men who are left alone.

'You are finding it difficult, sir?' I asked.

'Yes, very difficult David,' he replied honestly.

'Okay, here's my mobile number. Give me a call and we'll arrange it.'

Bev and her dad looked a little happier.

'Thanks so much David, thanks.'

'Thank you,' I replied and they left.

Sure enough, the very next day Bev rang and booked an appointment to come along and see me on Monday, 7th June. As I spoke to Bev, I had the most strange experience. I could actually see a lady smiling at me in my mind's eye.

'Bev. Your mum. This is your mum I can see in my mind.'

'Is it?' Bev asked. 'Is it really?' Again in disbelief.

I described Bev's mum's appearance to her over the phone.

'Oh my God,' she exclaimed. 'It is her.'

'And now she's showing me her lovely manicured pink nails, Bev'.

'She has always had her nails manicured and always had the colour pink,' she exclaimed.

After a while her mum began to mingle with the other thoughts my imagination was providing me with. Bev and I ended the phone call. Bev sounded so excited. I knew just how uplifted her spirits were as a result of what I had told her.

As the weeks went by, Bev's mum would often appear to me, but only briefly. I felt that she was just letting me know that she wanted communication with her daughter and her husband and she didn't want me to forget that they had an appointment.

Time flies here on the Earth plane, which is why we should enjoy each day and always appreciate those we love because our earthly life is merely a moment in the grand scale of things.

On Sunday, 6th June, Bev's mum had been manifesting herself to me throughout the day, so you can imagine how relieved I was when Monday night finally came.

We sat around our table. Bev's dad looked nervous. I could see that they were desperate to hear from their beloved wife and mother.

'Can I write things down? You know, things that you say, David,' Bev asked. 'I've got a pen and some paper.'

'Yes, no problem at all,' I replied.

Whenever I'm approached to do a private sitting, I ask the person who sits in front of me to impart very little information. I have always believed that when a person pays a visit to a medium, that medium should be able to give sufficient evidence of life after death without needing a prompt from their client. A medium worth his (or her) salt will not ask questions, only make statements.

After explaining this briefly, I began.

'I have a lady who joins me now. An older lady, quite smart, with white fluffy hair. Irritatingly, I feel she wants to interfere with the sitting today. She seems a bit pushy.'

'Do you know who it is, David?' Bev's father enquired.

'It's your paternal grandmother, Bev.'

'What's she saying, David?' Bev's dad asked inquisitively.

'Well, at present it is more what she's doing,' I replied. 'It's as if she doesn't want me to communicate with your mum, Bev. She is blocking my vision because I know your mother is standing behind her. I feel that this lady, sir, would have come between you and your wife in life.'

Bev's dad replied, 'Yes. Aye, she lived with us for a short while and what you're saying sounds typical of her.'

'I'm going to ask her to stand aside for a moment, so I am able to communicate with your mum. Stand to the side,' I said politely, 'I need to communicate with the lady behind you.'

I could feel the lady's reluctance to do this. I knew she didn't like the idea of not being the focus of our attention. Gradually, she moved out of my sight, but I could still sense her presence strongly.

Another lady joined me who I felt wanted to help Bev's mother. I told Bev that I thought it was another grandmother link.

'Can you ask her her name, David?' Bev's father asked.

'It's Ida, your mum's mum, Bev.'

'Oh my God,' Bev replied. 'We were just saying in the car, if you get my maternal grandmother's name, Ida, we would know you are really in touch – because it is an unusual name.'

'Your mum's here now Bev', I said.

'Can you see her?' Bev asked.

'Yes. She looks lovely. She is in a smart suit and her hair is nice and she is smiling. What's your name love?' I asked Bev's mum, but there was no reply.

'She's not answering me Bev.'

'Have you a name, my dear?' I asked again.

'Should I tell you her name, David?' Bev's dad asked.

'No, no, don't do that. Let me tell you,' I said firmly.

'That's why we've come to David, dad. Let him find out,' Bev insisted.

'Ida's calling out the name "Joan", so this name will mean something to you both.'

'That's my mum's name,' Bev affirmed.

'Yes, that's my wife's name,' Bev's dad said.

Next Ida shouted out "Michael" and communicated to me an image of *my* brother, John, thereby inferring that Michael is Bev's brother.

'The name Michael will also be relevant to you both,' I said, 'and I believe he is your brother, Bev.'

'Oh, God yes. He is my brother. How do you get that. I can't believe it. You have got his name too.'

'Amazing,' Bev's dad exclaimed.

Bev's grandmother was gradually making her way back into the focus of my inner vision.

'Roy, Roy,' she said.

'Roy. That's the name I'm being given now,' I said. 'Again from Ida, not from your mum.'

'That's me. I'm Roy,' Bev's dad exclaimed. 'That's me. That's my name'

Bev began to explain, 'I didn't give you dad's name. We did that on purpose. We thought that if my mum did come through she would tell you. Please don't think we doubted your ability.'

'No, we never doubted you could do this, David,' Bev's dad interjected. 'It's just, … you need to be sure. You know what I mean? Because there are people out there who say they can do this and it is just a lot of rubbish. They are just conning people'

'I understand what you mean, Bev. If I were sitting in front of a medium myself, I would be exactly the same as you. However, what I don't understand is why your mum is not communicating herself. I'll tell you what, I'll ask my guide, Jason, if there is a reason why your mum isn't communicating with me.'

'Okay then,' Bev agreed.

'Jason, could you step forward please,' I said.

A very familiar man appeared smiling before my mind's eye.

'Hi, Jason. Bev's mum's not communicating. Why is that?'

Jason explained that Joan hadn't been long in the World of Spirit and although she was very evolved for the length of time she *had* been there, she would need to be there a little longer to be able to communicate well. Jason then said he would help her during this session. I thanked him and explained to Bev and Roy what Jason had said.

My Spirit guide, Jason, is wonderful. Not only is he a great source of spiritual knowledge and understanding, but the help and protection that he provides me with when I am in need makes him my most valuable asset in my role as a medium.

I am clairvoyant, clairaudient and clairsentient, which means that I can see my friends in the World of Spirit, I can hear their voices and sense them strongly. I am thus privileged to have a rare gift, since most mediums have only one or two of these senses.

'As I look at your mum, I am aware that she has a little boy at her side. A little angel. So you would understand when I say that this little soul was miscarried, Bev?'

'Yes,' Bev replied quietly.

'Well he's fine and he's with your mum.'

Ida, not wanting to be outdone, shouted the name "James".

'James will be a name associated with you,' I said confidently.

'Yes, my son,' Bev replied in disbelief.

'Now, Jason is telling me that your mum likes your new car, but I am being told that there is also a joke about a new car, Roy, and there is a picture of a three-piece suite being shown to me.'

Bev said. 'I have just got a new car. Can mum see it?'

Joan gave me a thumbs up. 'Yes. She likes it,' I replied.

'Aye, and I've got a new car too,' says Roy. 'She was always on to me that she wanted a new three-piece suite, but I always said I wanted a new car and it became a standing joke in our house.'

Roy looked at me in disbelief.

'Your mum's showing me a sign for London, so there is a connection with London too.'

'Yes, yes, we understand that,' Bev said.

'Aye, yes we do,' replied Roy.

'Now I've got another gentleman standing at the side of Joan. He is smoking a pipe and he tells me that his name is "Jack" and he passed to the World of Spirit with a heart problem.'

'That's right,' said Roy. 'That's Joan's dad, Jack.'

'He's just coming forward to say he's keeping his eye on her and she is doing fine,' I said.

'Joan is now showing me a Starbuck's coffee shop and a sign saying "Macy's Department Store". She is sending me the number 9 and the number 11. Oh! You didn't have anyone injured or killed in the tragedy in America?' I exclaimed.

'No,' said Bev. 'But I know what mum means. We visited New York in December and she had her picture taken outside a Starbuck's coffee shop. We shopped in Macy's.' Bev began to go quiet.

'Would January be significant?' I asked.

'That's when she died,' Roy said sadly.

The image of Joan began to fade a little. I know from experience that when this happens, usually the Spirit person's energy is beginning to diminish.

I became aware of a lovely feeling of warmth in my heart. 'Your mum's going to have to go now, but she sends her love to you both and indeed all her family.'

'Bye, mum,' said Bev.

'I'll see you love,' Roy said quietly.

'Jason's telling me your mum will be able to communicate much better the next time you come along.'

'How long should that be?' Roy said.

'Well Roy, I'd leave it until after August. It will give Joan time to get used to her new surroundings, but you've had some great evidence haven't you? Most importantly, evidence that she's absolutely fine in the Spirit World. She is very happy,' I confirmed.

'Yes. Ida and my Grandad, Jack. I couldn't believe it when they came through,' said Bev.

Then Roy spoke up.

'No, it was quite remarkable, David, I must admit. I have never believed in anything like this before, but I do now. How would you know all that information – we are complete strangers to you?'

'Well, where there's love, there's life Roy. I hope it has been of some comfort to you both. I know Joan's crossing has left a massive void in both of your lives.'

'It has,' Bev replied. 'You always wonder where they are and if they're alright. You just want to know they're okay and they are not alone. I would hate to think of my mum being alone. She would not like that at all.'

'She isn't alone Bev, there is definite evidence of that.'

'So David, how did she know about the new cars? Had she been watching?'

'Oh yes. They like to check that we're okay and see what we're up to, just as they did when they were here on the Earth plane.

Remember Roy, when people cross over to the other side they don't suddenly change into spooks with chains hanging around their necks and their wrists, moaning and groaning. They are the same, minus the physical body. So, for instance, any health problems they experienced here on the Earth plane, they will be free from when they cross over, but their personality remains exactly the same.'

'Wow, it's marvellous when you think,' Roy said.

'It is,' Bev agreed.

'There you go, it's just another one of life's fantastic mysteries,' I said.

'We've taken enough of your time. Thanks, it's been brilliant,' Bev remarked.

'Yes, thanks David,' Roy said.

'You're welcome.'

I showed them to the door and wished them a safe journey. Nothing can compare with the sense of satisfaction I feel when I have successfully communicated with the Spirit world and watched their loved ones here on Earth experience the sense of love, joy and inner peace that communication brings. I regard my gift as a precious treasure which I have vowed to use for the good of others.

Months later, Bev telephoned me, interested to find out when our next demonstration would be and where it was going to be held. As I was talking to her over the phone my attention was diverted to my inner vision where her mother had begun to image herself strongly.

'Bev, your mum's just joined me,' I said.

'Has she?' said Bev, astonished.

'She has shown me a sign for Penwortham. Would you understand why?' I asked.

'Yes, that's where she lived,' Bev replied.

'Now she's showing me a bungalow, Bev. Did she live in one?'

'That's correct,' Bev said.

'She's wants me to ask you to tell your father that he's smoking too much and he must stop smoking in bed. Do you understand?'

Bev said, 'I'll certainly tell him. He's coming over for dinner tonight. Tell mum not to worry about that.'

'I've asked her if she has any more messages, Bev, and she's given me someone's nickname, "Capper".'

'That's my son's nickname. Everyone calls him Capper. That is amazing,' she exclaimed.

'Now your mother is impressing upon me that one of your brothers has asked your dad to lend him some money. She doesn't want your father to do this. Your brother had money last month and he hasn't given it back yet.'

'Your mother is showing me a Star of David and she's telling me that it's one of two such, but I can see this one on a lady. I can't quite grasp your mum's meaning, but she keeps repeating – *it's on a lady.*'

'I know exactly what she means. The Star is draped over a framed photograph of my mother at my brother's house and what's more David, there are definitely two of these Stars,' Bev confirmed.

'Bev, your mother wants you to know that she loves you very much.'

Bev seemed really happy. 'I wouldn't have thought you would be able to do that – give me a reading over the phone,' she commented.

'It doesn't make any difference at all,' I told her. 'Your mum just wanted to reassure you that she is alright.'

'Do you know, it's really strange, she's been on my mind a lot this week,' Bev said.

'Well, maybe she needed you to make this call so that she could give you this message through me. Perhaps she's worried about your father smoking too much and damaging his health. She's probably had her eye on him,' I said.

'That's just like my mother,' Bev replied.

After this phone conversation, I stood gazing out of my living room window at the ducklings swimming around in the pond. Completely out of the blue, a voice said, 'Well, you've made somebody's day, David.'

I turned round, but there was nobody else in the room.

Early the following year, I had received a telephone call from Bev who wanted to know if she and Roy could come to me for another sitting. She said her father had been greatly cheered by our last meeting. I gave her a booking.

On the appointed evening as I waited for Roy and Bev, the image of Beverley's mother Joan began to appear in my mind's eye. At about 7 o'clock, I began to wonder why they hadn't yet arrived. I opened my Appointments Diary to check that I hadn't got the wrong day or time. As I glanced down the page, my attention was attracted by Bev's mother who suddenly impressed,

They're stuck in traffic, just outside of Preston.

'Thanks, Joan,' I said out loud. 'Have I time for a coffee?'

Yes, Joan impressed on me.

A little later the doorbell rang – it was Bev and Roy.

'We're sorry we're late ...' began Bev.

'Don't worry,' I said. 'You've been stuck in traffic just outside Preston. Your mum's just told me.'

They both shot me a startled glance, then looked at one another.

I decided to seat them in the conservatory which is a less formal setting than my office. It has a pleasant, airy atmosphere and it's possible to feel at one with nature there.

When they had settled themselves, I started. 'Joan has joined us.' She began to impress information upon me.

'Harry Chadwick has passed away,' I said to Roy. Roy looked blank. 'I'll have to think about that one, David,' he said. 'I think I know who she means.'

'Bev. Your mum is telling me to keep your eye on Heather. You've been telling her off recently and your mum's pleased about this.'

'Yes,' Bev replied. 'I have.'

'Also, she wants you to know, Roy, that you will be doing something different this Christmas.'

'Yes, I will,' Roy replied. 'Do you want me to tell you what that is David?' he asked.

'No, no don't Roy. Joan's also telling me that you have been doing something different on Friday nights.'

Roy looked sheepish at this last disclosure.

'A lovely black and white dog has just come to sit down beside your mother, Bev. Your mum is showing me a penny and twirling it around.'

'Goodness!' exclaimed Bev.   'That's our dog, she was called "Penny".'

'And she's saying that she's seen aunty Margaret too, her brother's wife, who is still on the Earth plane. Do you understand?'

'Yes we do definitely,' Bev confirmed.

I turned back to Roy. 'Joan's talking about your having a meal out on Friday night at a pub. I can't quite get the name of the pub, but Joan is transmitting an image of it to me – and it's a big, white, old building.'

'Yes,' replied Roy. He looked distinctly uneasy.

'Who's "Pat", Roy? Joan is giving me the name "Pat".' Roy and Bev both seemed shocked.

'It's someone I've been seeing, David – a friend. Is Joan angry with me?' he asked quietly.

'No Roy. She's happy for you,' I replied. Joan was communicating to me that she didn't mind at all; she was in fact rather glad that Roy had begun to go out again. Since her death, he had spent most of his time watching television or visiting Bev's house. Joan pointed out that Pat was good company for Roy. I sensed that Joan had known her here on Earth and liked her. Roy confirmed that they had been friends. He appeared overjoyed at Joan's reaction.

'Pat has been married twice, Joan's telling me,' I went on.

'That's correct,' Roy said.

'She's telling me that Pat is quite soft and gentle whereas she, Joan, was a little stronger character – more to the point.'

'That's very true,' Roy acknowledged.

'You've been discussing going away on holiday just recently.'

'Yes,' Roy replied.

'Joan wants you to go. She would like you to show Pat all the places that you went to together when she was here.'

Roy asked me to thank Joan for him. But Joan impressed upon me that she had a further message for Roy.

'Now Joan says that there is an "Alan" connection to Pat.'

Roy nodded.

'And a sixtieth birthday coming up. That's a November celebration and there's going to be a party.'

'This is all true, David,' said Roy, astonished. 'Is Joan telling you this?'

'Of course, Roy. How else would I know?' I smiled.

'Now Bev. She likes the shoes you are wearing, you got them when you were on holiday.'

'Yes, yes I did,' Bev replied.

'Joan is beginning to step back now,' I told them.

'David. Could you ask her a question?' Roy asked.

'Yes,' I replied.

'Does she know that my love for her is still as strong as it ever was?'

Joan held up a big red love heart which made me smile and I was able to assure Roy that indeed she *did* know, and was happy that he was no longer overcome with grief.

'Joan is going now,' I said, 'but she wants you both to know that she loves you and asks to be remembered to all the family.'

Roy said urgently, 'David, I need to ask another question.'

'Fire away Roy,' I said.

'When I die, if I'm still with Pat – I like Pat a lot, she's a lovely, lovely lady – what will happen to me? Will I be with Pat or Joan on the other side?'

I could understand Roy's concern and I was aware of his thoughts behind his question.

Joan pictured on holiday on Malta in September, 1989.

'You will be with both Roy. Joan understands. She likes Pat. If you've been happy with Pat on the Earth then you will be with her and with Joan and with all the people you've loved.'

'Marvellous!' Roy replied. 'It's as if a weight has been lifted off my shoulders.'

'He's been feeling guilty,' Bev explained. 'Because he was with my mum all those years, he needed to know she didn't mind, you know, about his having another relationship.'

'You understand David, don't you?' Roy said.

I replied that I did.

As they prepared to leave, they thanked me profusely and it was a great satisfaction to me to see their pleasure.

I still find it difficult to accept that I can communicate with the World of Spirit. Each time I finish a demonstration, or a private sitting, I have to convince myself that I've actually done what I *have* done. I believe that my guides and helpers are making sure that my feet are kept firmly on the ground and I can understand why.

It would be easy, in the circumstances, for me to be carried away with my own importance. However, because I have been given such a gift, it would be unforgivable of me to forget that the gift is *given* and not the result of merit on my own part.

Chapter 9

The Learning Curve

The more I used my spirit abilities, the more my gift began to grow. I decided to put an advert in the local paper announcing that I was available to do private readings. At this time, I was already making some stage appearances and doing spirit readings for friends, but I felt strongly that I ought to be doing more. The newspaper came out on the Wednesday and by Thursday I was inundated with phone calls...

My first client gave her name as "Mrs Weaver". She arrived at my home one Wednesday evening. As I opened my front door, a tall, thin lady, nervously clutching her handbag to her chest, stood on the doorstep.

'Mrs Weaver?' I said smiling.

'Christine. Please call me "Christine",' she replied pleasantly.

'Come in Christine,' I said.

As she stepped into the hall she stared at me without blinking. Her eyes were almost popping out of her head. 'I've seen Jesus!' she exclaimed. I looked at her and smiled.

'Now where did that come from?' I asked.

She just smiled and said nothing more.

I ushered her into my office and offered her a drink, which she declined.

I started the reading somewhat apprehensively, startled by Christine's strange remark and her vacant expression.

'Now Christine, as I sit in front of you I am asking my guides to give me information which will relate to you. If you understand what I say and it makes sense, please just say "yes". Do you understand?' I queried.

Christine smiled. 'Can I ask you a question first please?' she asked politely.

'Yes go ahead,' I replied, still wondering about what she might say.

Christine took a long deep breath, then turned away for a moment, before finally facing me. Slowly releasing the air in her lungs and smiling, she began, 'I was woken up one night by a noise outside my house. As I opened my eyes, a man stood watching me at the foot of my bed. He said his name was Jesus of Nazareth. My room was filled with white light. Since this happened my whole life has changed. I've lost my husband to another woman, I've had a nervous breakdown. Do you think I'm going mad?' she asked directly.

'No', I said softly, 'but what I can say to you, Christine, if it is of any help, is that when I tell people about my experiences it must cross their minds that *I'm* mad. You shouldn't worry about anyone else's opinion – maybe it's time for you to move forward, leave your experience behind you, start afresh.'

Still staring at me, Christine said, 'I'll go now, I've got what I came for David.'

'Good,' I said. 'It was lovely meeting you Christine and I hope to see you again sometime. God Bless.' As I opened my front door, Christine turned around and laughed loudly, pointing her finger at me as if I'd cracked a joke. I smiled and closed the door, considerably unnerved.

Barry and Andrea sat watching the television in the living room.

'How did it go?' Barry asked. He scanned my face and remarked, 'That bad!'

'No, not bad, just different,' I replied.

I settled down to enjoy my evening meal, my mind still on the strange encounter I had had with Christine.

My confidence was a little shaken.

Later, I joined the others in the lounge. We chatted about the happenings of the day, then the doorbell rang.

'Subject number two!' Barry announced laughing.

'Good luck!' Andrea added, giving me a kiss.

I answered the door this time to a smart, middle-aged lady dressed in a navy blue suit. She wore glasses and her hair had golden highlights.

'Hello, I'm Margaret,' she said.

'I'm David. Do come in.'

Thanking me she made her way into the hall and followed me to my office.

I offered her the usual tea or coffee to put her at her ease.

'No thanks I'm fine,' she replied.

I explained to her how I like to work and then turned my attention to my guide Jason. When Jason is here, I can sense his presence. He is a great comfort and a source of confidence to me.

'The name 'Michael' is being given to me by my guide,' I began.

'Yes I understand,' she said nervously.

It was being impressed upon me to say that Michael hadn't been well of late, in fact he'd been quite ill. After I had given this information to Margaret, she became upset immediately, tears flooding from her eyes.

'He's going to die David. Is he going to die? Do you mean he's going to die?' she demanded to know.

'No, no Margaret', I tried to reassure her, 'I've not said that.' She began to calm down, wiping tears from her eyes. 'You would understand an important anniversary, a birthday, in April?' I asked.

'Yes I do David, my birthday's in April,' Margaret replied.

'The 21st?'

'Correct,' she said.

'Also June. There is another birthday in June,' I went on.

'Yes it's Michael's.' She began to cry again.

'June 20th?' I retorted.

'Yes, oh yes, oh! He's going to die, I know he's going to die.' She continued to cry. 'David please tell me he's not.'

She was so distressed, I desperately wanted to reassure her. 'No, he's not going to die,' I said firmly. Then I added with conviction, 'He's probably going to be out with his mates next Friday night, having a few pints, letting his hair down, enjoying himself.'

Margaret looked shocked. 'But David, he's a *cat!*' she said.

I looked at her in horror. The atmosphere in the room changed completely and we both burst out laughing.

'Well Margaret,' I said, 'that's one I possibility I never anticipated.'

'David, I needed cheering up, it's the best laugh I've had in ages, thank you so much.'

The reading had come to a natural conclusion and so had I. After saying goodbye to Margaret, I sat down alone with my thoughts. As I turned my focus to my inner vision I saw Jason, smiling. 'Why did that go so wrong?' I asked. 'You weren't *asking* me for information,' Jason impressed upon me. 'You were waiting for me to give you evidence and then using the evidence to form your own conclusion. If you want to form your own conclusions, why do you need me as a guide?'

I was obviously being taught one of the many lessons I have learnt on my spiritual path. I thanked Jason for his wisdom and made the decision that night to ask his help or that of any other spirit guide who chose to work with me. I wouldn't jump to conclusions and would impart information as it was given to me, whether it made sense to me or not.

It was half way through the year and about half way through my calendar of demonstrations when I found myself in sunny Liverpool.

I love the people there. They are always smiling. I thoroughly enjoy the bravado and banter that is characteristic of my demonstrations in that city.

On this particular evening, the demonstration had started well with my forming a link with a gentleman in spirit who gave his name as "Joseph Wilson" and his place of abode on the Earth as "Fazakerley".

At this demonstration, the seats were not arranged in rows but, more informally, around small tables. The sound of a female voice calling loudly 'Here David!' drew my attention to a table at which a group of women were sitting. The attractive lady who had spoken had long blonde hair, round glasses, wore a white T-shirt and jeans.

'This gentleman says he wants to speak to his wife, Margaret, and daughters Lorraine and Sue.'

'That's us,' confirmed another of the ladies seated at the same table. Her voice was tremulous and she seemed near to tears.

'Joe had lung cancer and when the diagnosis was made, he asked Margaret to promise him that she would let him die at home. She kept her promise and Joe wants to thank her,' I relayed.

Joe passed on his love and thanks. He was particularly concerned about his wife who had been battling with depression since his death. Margaret seemed astounded by what I had told her. Her companions at the demonstration, who were members of her family, were also overwhelmed. They were all particularly emotional when I passed on from Joe the poignant piece of information that his daughter's four-year-old son, James, was with him in the Spirit World.

James had had leukaemia and had died twelve months previously.

As Joe began to leave, he indicated another spirit figure, a man he said he knew here on the Earth. The man's name was "Ed". Joe continued to fade and Ed's form became clearer.

He began by informing me that he was an enthusiastic Everton F.C. supporter. Ironically, he had had a heart attack whilst watching an Everton match on television, some years previously. Just as I located his family in the audience, there was a massive explosion which seemed to have come from somewhere in the road outside the club. The building shook violently. Then there was a second explosion, as loud as the first. After their initial shock, members of the audience began to rush around in all directions, a good number of them to the windows, to ascertain the source of the explosions. Some became hysterical. People lit up cigarettes, switched on their mobile phones and began trying to contact their families. Within seconds we could hear the sound of police sirens. Helicopters filled the sky.

One of the officials at the club came towards me. 'Could you make an announcement please, Dave?' he said. 'The Police have insisted that no one should leave the building.'

I made the announcement and many people returned to their seats. I decided to carry on with my demonstration of clairvoyance but Ed had obviously moved on, perhaps because of the enormousness of the explosion. The demonstration concluded at 10.30pm. There was cheering and whistling from the audience, partly, I think, because people appreciated the fact that Barry and I had carried on regardless, after a rumour had flown around the club that a terrorist bombing had occurred.

Driving home was an absolute nightmare. All the roads were blocked off. Police stopped every vehicle and interviewed all drivers, asking such questions as where they had come from and where they were travelling to. The next day all was revealed. As I was driving to work, I clicked on my car radio which reported that someone had filled a car with fireworks, parked it outside a local police station, which just happened to be next door to the club where we were conducting our demonstration, and set fire to the car – that was the first explosion. The fireworks caused the second. Luckily, no one was hurt. I felt this was yet another test of fate. Liverpool had definitely gone with a bang!

The Spirits were to test me again that very evening. I had previously been asked to demonstrate my clairvoyance at a countryside inn on the outskirts of Wigan. I was reluctant to do so and thus I had refused.

However, during my meditation that night Jason, my guide, made it clear to me that he wanted me to take on the demonstration. So, accordingly, I contacted the landlady and, with a marked lack of enthusiasm, told her that I had changed my mind. She seemed pleased with my decision and said that some of her friends and customers had mentioned my clairvoyance and she was intrigued.

So, the night after the explosion in Liverpool, Barry and I made our way to the country pub to demonstrate. When we arrived, the room was not at all what I'd expected. It's most obvious drawbacks were that it was positively tiny and had no door. A young boy from behind the bar approached me and said the landlady had instructed him to pin a curtain over the entrance to reduce the level of noise – which was increasing as we spoke – from the public bar. Negativity set in instantly. When this happens, my best bet is usually not to attempt connections with the Spirit World. Barry insisted, however, that we try to make the best of the situation, and in addition, I was swayed by Jason's request that I give a demonstration there. Whenever he specifically asks me to do this, it is usually because someone is desperate for a message from the Spirit World and that message is invariably forthcoming.

The room began to fill and by eight o'clock it was like a sweat-shop. I was obliged to stand on the kerb around the fireplace in order to be visible to members of the audience furthest away from me. I threw open the windows to let in some cool air and started my demonstration. Although I knew the messages I was receiving were spirit-given and not my imagination playing tricks, strangely, no one in the audience responded when I asked if anyone could 'take' a message.

The temperature in the room was rising and the noise from the bar was becoming overbearing. A couple of grown men, around the age of 60, skipped back and forth across the entrance emitting "woo-ing" noises to simulate ghosts. It was the final straw when one silly old man tapped on the window and shouted 'Is there anybody there?' Calmly and directly, I caught the eye of the landlady. 'If I don't get a little respect for what I'm doing there will be a lot of disappointed customers this evening,' I said incisively. She immediately called for order in the bar area. The noise died down a little but I was on a negative road to nowhere. I couldn't concentrate in the airless room, which made me feel stifled and cornered. There were too many people in such a confined space. I stopped and asked the audience if anyone had any objection to sitting outside in the car park.

'No,' they all replied.

It was a lovely, starry night and we all picked up our chairs and went outside. I demonstrated clairvoyance under the stars making strong links with the Spirit World. My audience listened with great attention. At around 10.30 I called it a night, thanking all the people for bearing with me. They all agreed that the room was inappropriate for a clairvoyant demonstration. The lady whom I had first approached in the stuffy room came over to me. She said she had understood everything I'd said to her, that it was all correct and true, but that she had not wanted to have her business and private affairs mentioned in front of her friends. Tired and stressed by all the experiences of the last two days, I could only comment 'Well my love, I *did* say at the beginning of my demonstration that I would not reveal anyone's private business.' The woman's daughter acknowledged this to be true and led her mother away. However, we parted on good terms.

I had been taught another valuable lesson by the spirits, which was that I should never agree to conduct a demonstration at a venue which I had not first seen. My next evening of clairvoyance took place in my home-town of St. Helens where I have always been well-received. I think it's because I'm a local lad.

I was feeling on top form and as I opened the demonstration with my usual introductions, I looked over my shoulder and saw that Barry was already sketching away. I was just about to speak to the audience when I was made aware of a smartly-dressed little old lady walking towards me. Her coat was classically well-cut and she wore toning beige shoes and carried a matching handbag.

Mediums should possess the ability to communicate with spirit individuals and members of the audience simultaneously. This may seem a difficult accomplishment, but all mediums will acknowledge that it is absolutely necessary.

As I carried on talking to my audience I asked the spirit lady her name. *Lillian Unsworth*, she replied in a beautiful cultured voice.

Where did you live when you were on the earth plane Lillian? I asked.

At St. Helens. I'm a Lancashire lass, she replied smiling.

I asked Lillian to stay with me and she agreed.

'Now my first friend has joined me from the World of Spirit, her name is "Lillian Unsworth" and she is from St. Helens.' Then I described the lady's physical appearance and clothing and tried to give some impression of her voice.

'David, I think Lillian Unsworth has come along to speak to me,' a tall lady called from the back of the audience.

'Lillian is telling me that she is your grandmother,' I continued.

'She is,' the lady asserted.

A lovely message followed from Lillian, which was filled with evidence from the Spirit World. The next link worried me. A gentleman joined me from the World of Spirit, again giving me his full name, "William Matthews". He told me he had died when he was 62 years old from a heart attack, the last in a series he had had. He said he had connections with Rainford and Southport and added that his wife was there in the audience. After describing his physical appearance and relaying all the information he'd given me, I was totally astounded when no one would "accept" the gentleman, so I asked him for some more information. He obliged by giving me the names of his sons, Andrew and Gerard, the name of his daughter-in-law, Judith and that of his grandson, Simon. Still the room was silent.

I usually ask an audience no more than three times and if the name or description of a spirit with whom I am in contact is not recognized, I ask the spirit to step back. This gentleman looked upset so I asked him if there was something wrong. There was. He was worried about his son Gerard and he desperately wanted to speak to his wife but she obviously would not acknowledge him.

Again, I gave his name and personal details to the audience, but no one replied. Looking disappointed, the gentleman left quietly. It is not often that anything like this happens to me but when it does, I am always disappointed on behalf of the person in spirit and convinced that my audience will believe that I have made everything up.

At the end of the evening, after the demonstration, Barry and I received rapturous applause.

Chapter 10

Bill and Maureen

The next day I was late for work as usual. It was a quarter past nine when I burst through the salon door exclaiming, 'Traffic's terrible Josie'. Josie looked up and laughed.

'It's okay I'm doing my crossword,' she joked.

I threw my coat off and collected a big mug of coffee from Sue. The phone began to ring. Jayne at the reception desk called, 'David it's for you.'

Apologizing to Josie and joking that she should be out of the salon by lunchtime, I went to take the call.

'Hello?'

'David?' queried a voice at the other end of the line, 'My name's Maureen Gray and you don't know me but I was at the clairvoyant demonstration the other night in St. Helens.'

I could sense tension in Maureen's voice.

'I hope you are not ringing to ask me for your money back,' I joked.

The joke had its effect in breaking the ice. Maureen laughed aloud and began to speak openly.

'Not at all,' she said. 'In fact, I was really really thrilled. I enjoyed the whole evening. I was talked into going by my friend Margaret, a client at one of your salons. I must admit I was sceptical...'. Here she paused a moment '...until you gave me a message. It was from my first husband. Do you remember, David?'

I don't have the best memory in the world I must admit and since I started to communicate with the Other Side, it seems to have become worse. Either that or I'm really a 79-year-old man in a 39-

year-old body! The point of the matter was that I couldn't remember the particular communication Maureen was talking about. I had to confess this to her, adding that because the information had passed through me, it was not a part of my own memory. Also, that I had had such a large number of links at the demonstration, it was difficult to remember them all.

'My husband's name was William Matthews, Bill. He was concerned about my son Gerard. You *must* remember David!'

Of course, I did now! I gently asked Maureen why she had chosen to remain silent when I had repeatedly offered the name "William Matthews". I told her I was sad on the spirit's behalf when no one acknowledged him, especially as he seemed so worried. I went on to say that most people who attend clairvoyant demonstrations do so with the hope of being able to participate.

'I am sorry about that,' Maureen said. 'I have phoned this morning to explain to you why I didn't acknowledge Bill. He and I had two sons. When our second was born, Bill changed. He became violent, sometimes even brutal, towards us and I feared for the children's lives. So, one night whilst he was out drinking in the town, I packed as many of our belongings as I could and with the children asleep in their pram, I left the house. Eventually, I made my way to Dublin where I stayed with a great aunt. I went there because I thought Bill did not know of her existence.

'Three years later, my mother became ill and I returned to England. Bill had met some other unlucky woman. I was glad. Mum died in my arms two weeks later. The day after her death, Bill came to where I was staying. He wanted a divorce. I agreed, of course.

'I worked hard David, to bring up my boys. I met my second husband Robert and my boys call him "dad". He's been a rock, a great source of strength and support. So you can understand why I didn't acknowledge Bill.' She hesitated a moment, then added, 'I have rung to apologise to you and I need to know something David.'

I enquired what it was.

'Is it true that when we cross to the World of Spirit, we learn by the mistakes we made on earth?'

'We do Maureen. We are always learning in this life and in the After Life.'

'Maybe Bill's changed, maybe he's learned,' Maureen said pensively.

'It would not be the first time a husband in the Spirit World has requested me to pass on his apologies to his wife. Maybe that is what Bill wanted to do last night.'

There was silence at the other end of the phone. I went on, 'But if you had acknowledged him, we wouldn't be guessing, would we?'

'I hope he has changed,' Maureen said quietly.

I thanked her for letting me know that Bill had been her husband and we said "goodbye".

I glanced across at Josie who was waiting patiently for me to begin work on her hair.

'Sorry Josie love,' I said.

She smiled and joked, 'Problems again?'

Some weeks later, Margaret came into the salon.

'David, can I have a word with you,' she said, beckoning me over to the corner of the room. 'I just wanted you to know that Gerard, Maureen's son, has died suddenly at home of a massive heart attack. He had had no prior warning that there was anything wrong. Maureen is suffering from shock. The night after she had telephoned you to explain about her husband, Bill, we both went to the Spiritualist Church in St. Helens. Bill tried to come through the medium there to speak to her. But again, she could not bring herself to acknowledge him. The medium repeated that Bill was worried about his son, Gerard. In addition to her terrible grief about Gerard's death,

Maureen feels guilty because she thinks Bill was trying to warn her about Gerard's heart attack and if she had been willing to acknowledge Bill, she might have saved Gerard.'

A tear fell from Margaret's eye.

'Would you like me to telephone Maureen?' I asked gently.

'I'd be grateful if you would,' said Margaret. I promised to do so.

That night, I contacted Maureen and tried to comfort her. At the end of our conversation, she said she felt better about the whole situation. She was anxious for me to try to contact Gerard for her at a later date and I agreed to do this. As we said our parting "goodbyes", I clearly heard a man's voice saying, *Tell "Duck Egg" I'm fine. I've made it. I live.* I repeated the words to Maureen.

'Gerard is the only person in the whole world who called me "Duck Egg",' she told me. 'I'm overjoyed. Thank you David, thank you from the bottom of my heart.'

Chapter 11

Troublesome George

As well as demonstrating my spirit gifts in hotels and theatres, I am sometimes requested to demonstrate in Spiritualist Centres. One such occasion that was particularly memorable for me occurred in a Spiritualist Centre near Blackpool, where I encountered "George".

As I have already stated, before I conduct a demonstration I meditate. This allows my mind to settle down and focus. As may be imagined, a busy day in a hairdressing salon can be tiring and stressful. It is important for me as a medium, to leave the day's events behind and still my mind. During these meditations, it is often the case that one or two of the departed loved ones of prospective members of the audience, at that evening's demonstration, will materialize or connect with me in some other way. It did not happen on this occasion.

Barry and I arrived twenty minutes early and, after the usual introductions, we were led down a long corridor into a side room where we were offered a drink by a charming, smiling lady. She said she would leave us to meditate and would come back to call us when we were required to begin the demonstration. We thanked her.

Barry sat down and put his head back, closing his eyes. 'You're not falling asleep, I hope,' I said.

'No. I'm trying to meditate,' he replied.

Closing my eyes, I attempted to quieten my own mind, requesting my guides and helpers to help anyone who wanted communication from the higher side of life to come forward. No sooner had I done this than a man in his late sixties appeared in my mind's eye. He had smart, wiry, grey hair and large yellow teeth. He began to smile politely.

Hello sir, I said.

He introduced himself as "George", in a voice which was crystal clear.

Have you come along for anyone in the audience tonight? I asked.

Yes. Maureen, he replied.

I enquired what circumstances had led to his being in the World of Spirit?

Cancer. Lung cancer, he answered.

I am sorry to hear that, I told him. I like to let my spirit friends know that I care about their welfare. I believe they sense this when they communicate with me.

Having received this information from George, I requested him to be available if his loved ones in the audience wanted to contact him.

I opened my eyes and Barry stood looking out of the window.

'Were you talking to someone?' he asked.

'Yes,' I replied. 'I've got my first link. He's a ...'

'Please don't tell me,' Barry interrupted.

'Okay, I'm sorry,' I replied. I could see George in my mind's eye. He was as plain as day.

I had the very strange feeling that there was something not quite right with this communication. I decided to cut my link with George but for some reason could not do so.

Barry nudged me, 'I think we're on now,' he announced.

The door opened slowly and the familiar face of Margaret gently peeked in. 'Okay boys?' she asked.

'Fine,' Barry replied.

Margaret entered clasping a clip-board, from which she read out to us the evening's agenda. Then she led us out onto the stage. The hall was packed. A large man, formally dressed in suit and tie, announced us. There followed a rapturous applause and even a cheer or two – which was quite unmerited at this stage, since Barry and I had not even spoken yet. I introduced us both, explaining a little about the way we worked. Then I told the audience I would give a demonstration of clairvoyance.

Turning my attention to my mind's eye I could see George. *Are you ready George?* I asked.

I am ready, he replied.

Okay then, I said. *Let's go.* 'Now ladies and gentleman I have a man who joins me from the World of Spirit. He is in his sixties and has wiry, grey hair. He has strong, large teeth. I believe he crossed over with lung cancer. He tells me his name is George and his loved one in the audience is a lady called Maureen.'

Silence fell over the audience. No-one answered. 'George and Maureen,' I repeated. Still no one answered. Some members of the audience began to shuffle uncomfortably in their seats.

'I can take that.' Shouted a voice from the back of the hall.

'Hello,' I said. The lady smiled but did not reply. This was not helpful to me. A medium is dependent on voice vibrations from a recipient to help strengthen the links.

'Hello, my friend,' I projected my voice to the rear of the hall.

'Hello love,' a now timid voice replied.

'George is telling me that he is your uncle.'

'That's correct,' she replied.

'He says he was a businessman here on the Earth.'

'He was.'

'Since he crossed, his wife has met someone else and is very happy. She's rebuilding her life quite nicely now, since her sad loss.'

'That's right,' the lady replied, then in a rush of words she added, 'but she wasn't all that sad when George died. He was a mean old fart and she had the life of a dog with him.'

There was much muttering in the audience and one or two embarrassed titters. Then a profound silence in the hall.

'He was,' went on the woman. 'He was really mean with her, but since she's met Cyril her life is totally different.'

I turned my attention to George, wondering what his reaction might be.

We had a beautiful home, he said clearly. He began to project an image for me of a lovely, detached stone house.

'He tells me he and his wife had a lovely detached stone house.'

'They did. It was a bloody prison to my aunty,' the lady said sharply. 'Prison!' she emphasised.

George looked sad. *I'll go,* he said and when I looked again, he'd gone.

'George has left, but can I leave his love with you?' I asked her.

'I don't want his love,' she said bitterly. 'I don't want his love at all.'

Politely I thanked her for her communication and moved on quickly. As I picked up my next link, I watched the lady leave. Her exit left me feeling uncomfortable for the rest of the evening.

The rest of the demonstration was very successful. When it was over, many people walked over to Barry and me to thank us and comment on the accuracy of our evidence. Margaret brought tea and fresh cream scones for us. Although we didn't really want to eat, especially Barry who is a diabetic, Margaret was so insistent that I ate them both so we would not appear to be impolite.

As we journeyed home, Barry and I began to discuss the night's events. When I mentioned George, my attention was drawn to my inner vision. George's face met me. 'Hello George,' I said politely.

'Hello,' he answered.

'What can I do for you?'

'I've not talked to the right person,' he complained.

'Oh, but you wanted Maureen.'

'I want to speak to Gill my wife,' he insisted.

'But the demonstration's over now sir. It's time for you to leave.' George didn't reply but continued to obtrude himself into my inner vision.

When I arrived home I took myself off into my office to make sure that I "closed myself down" properly. Again, I asked George to leave but he wouldn't do so. It is difficult to convey what I am trying to say. However, I will try. When I was a child, television was not broadcast for 24 hours a day as now. BBC Television had a test card. It was a picture of a young girl with a cuddly toy on her lap holding a board with noughts and crosses on it. Older readers may remember it. Whenever that particular channel wasn't transmitting a programme, the test card would appear on the screen. My experience with George was rather like this.

It was midnight and he was still with me. Barry suggested that it could be my subconscious mind playing tricks, but I knew certainly that this was not the case. I began to get annoyed, not only with George, but also with Barry and Andrea for doubting me.

Another hour passed, Barry was asleep on the couch and Andrea on the armchair. I was still wide awake. I desperately attempted to contact Jason, my guide, but there was no response. Why had I lost control and where was my guide?

Without warning, George began to cry – and I began to cry too. I cried on and on. Andrea woke up. 'What's wrong David,' she asked anxiously.

'I don't know. George is crying and I'm feeling so emotional.' My bout of weeping continued until I had cried myself and Andrea, to sleep.

I awoke to the sound of my mobile phone playing its familiar *Torra Dance* ring tone. I hastily scrambled around for my wrist-watch. 'Oh no! Twenty past eight' I exclaimed. 'Hey, you two. We are going to be late.'

Andrea and Barry woke quickly, with familiar exclamations of dismay. One after another, we took hurried showers and set off for work.

We arrived fifteen minutes late but, to my intense relief, there was no George – until I set foot in the shop! I picked up my coffee and walked through into the salon area to apologise for being late to my first regular customer.

'George, what the hell are you doing here?' I exclaimed angrily.

'What did you say?' Maureen my client enquired. I had spoken to George aloud.

'Sorry Maureen. Talking to myself again. I need some help!' I joked.

Maureen laughed. As I blow dried her hair, she chatted away, but I was only half-listening to what she said. All the time, I was aware of the spirit man in my mind's eye. It was very, very annoying to me, so much so that by five o'clock I'd had enough. I decided I needed the help of Jim Roe, my mentor and the leader of the Development Circle that I attend weekly. He would know what to do.

That night I telephoned Jim but there was no answer. This situation also was very usual. Jim was always there, just in case anyone needed advice. Desperately, I rang another circle member who informed me that Jim's wife, Frances, had been rushed into hospital. Well, that settled that one.

It was 10:30pm and my mind and body were crying out for sleep.

George. Please leave me. I need to sleep, I begged, but in vain. There he remained.

Finally, in a fit of desperation, I was driven to yell out, *George! Your bloody wife couldn't stand you, your niece thought you were a tight old fart and now I'm bloody sick of you too.* I had never before used such abusive language to a spirit. George began to laugh.

I'm going nowhere, he announced. His voice was crystal clear. In anger and frustration, I began to bang my head violently on the dining room wall. Suddenly I stopped. This is a test, I thought. This has got to be a lesson. I looked at George and decided to try a different tack.

George, you can stay as long as you want to, I said. *I send my love to you.* George smiled, but he didn't move.

As I climbed into bed I closed my eyes and focused my attentions on the darkness at the back of my eyelids. Although I could still sense George's presence, I fell into a deep sleep.

I was woken at around 2:00am by the sound of my car alarm going off. I jumped up. Andrea had beaten me to it. She had run downstairs and collected the keys which we kept hidden in a drawer. She quickly turned off the noisy alarm.

'That's better,' I sighed.

'Go back to sleep love,' she urged.

I pulled the bed covers back over me and was irresistibly drawn to my inner vision. George was still there, smiling. *Still with us, George?* I asked. *God, bless you,* I added.

At 3:00am I was awoken again by my car alarm. Up I shot, tripping over my bedroom slippers. I'm not at my best when my sleep has been disturbed, I must admit. This time, the alarm stopped before I could get to it.

I'll do it again and again and again, George said clearly. I sat on the edge of the bed and broke down in tears.

'You! It was you all along,' I cried.

Yes, George said laughing.

Andrea turned to me. 'Is it the spirit gentleman?' she asked. 'Yes, it is, and tomorrow, I'm going to sort this out once and for all. I've had enough, Andrea.'

Andrea could see how annoyed and distressed I was. Putting her arms around me she cuddled me until I fell into a deep sleep.

During that night we were woken every hour by the too familiar sound of my car alarm. At 7:30 we were woken by a different alarm.

Andrea and I sat up in bed. She looked pale from lack of sleep and I expect I did too. Barry walked into the room with tea and coffee on a tray.

'Morning,' he said cheerfully. 'Well, you both look shattered.'

'We are,' Andrea replied. 'Didn't you hear the car alarm going off constantly?'

'Yes, a few times, but then I was so tired it just didn't trouble me after that,' he replied.

'You could sleep through a nuclear war,' Andrea joked.

'You both look terrible. Why don't you stay in bed and get some sleep,' Barry insisted.

I was tempted to do this but remembered I had a number of phone calls to make.

Andrea explained that she had far too many appointments booked for her to be able to take the day off and with that, the day started.

I was still unable to gain contact with Jim Roe and I desperately needed to do so. George was still with me. That morning I rang June, one of the leaders at the Purple Light Spiritual Centre in Chorley, and told her everything. I suspect she could tell by the tone of my voice how I was feeling.

'Why didn't you call me earlier,' June asked. 'It sounds as if your spirit friend is Earth-bound. He probably didn't want to leave his family, friends and home and he has just stayed around them instead of crossing over into the light. Now he's lost and, furthermore, he's attached himself to you because he knows that you can help him. You *can* rescue him David,' June said in a definite tone.

'Rescue him?' I exploded. 'It's I who need to be rescued!'

June explained how I could help George to pass into the light and I agreed to try. That night, after our evening meal, Andrea, Barry and I sat in a circle. We began with a prayer asking our guides to help us with the rescue. Then I turned my attention to my inner sight. George was still staring back at me. I began to talk to him, telling him he needed to cross into the light. George acknowledged me, but said nothing.

'Can you see the light George?' I asked him.

No, he replied. Then he stood up and began to look around. *No, there's just darkness David,* he said.

As he stood there a white dot appeared at his side and began to grow. The dot became brighter and brighter as it became a large circle. Eventually, its brightness was overwhelming. George looked at the circle and then at me. His eyes were filled with tears.

That's the light, isn't it, David? he said.

'Yes, that's it George. Now walk towards it and someone will meet you and help you cross over.'

George was reluctant at first. Then, after a little encouragement, he walked slowly towards the circle. An elderly lady walked from the circle of light and, just behind her, an elderly man.

Mother, George exclaimed. *It's my mother and father!* George's emotions were overwhelming. I was very moved and began to cry. I watched George hug his parents and walk with them arm in arm, into the light. The circle began to close and again my inner vision became dark.

I opened my eyes and looked at Barry and Andrea. They also had been very emotional. Then I thanked my guides for all their help. I was so relieved. It was a great weight off my mind.

I rang June immediately to tell her what had happened. 'Congratulations!' she said. 'You have just rescued your first spirit person. That's another lesson under your belt.'

As usual, the following week Barry and I attended our local Spiritualist Centre at Chorley. The speaker that night was a tutor from Stansted Hall, Essex. I have never been there myself but those who have, describe their visits as "spiritually uplifting".

After a rather interesting discourse about her philosophy of life, the medium gestured towards Barry. 'Sir, I'd like to come to you. I believe you are a psychic artist.'

'I am,' Barry replied.

'A gentleman, who was a policeman back in the early 'forties/ 'fifties, has joined me from the World of Spirit. He tells me you have his gold pocket watch. Do you understand, sir?' she asked.

'Yes, I do,' Barry said.

'He tells me he is very proud of you.'

Barry looked pleased, 'Thank you,' he replied.

'He tells me there have been many changes in your life which you have had to come to terms with. You have moved home to a different house and also your career has changed dramatically.'

'Yes, that's correct,' Barry said.

'He would just like you to know that he is near to you and that you have made the right decision in these changes.'

'Thank you,' Barry answered.

'Take his love,' she said. 'Now sir, I'd like to come to you.' The medium pointed to me. I smiled and nodded.

'Hello,' I said.

She too smiled and began, I have a message from the World of Spirit. George is fine. He is very happy. He wants to thank you for all you've done. Do you understand?'

'I understand completely,' I said. Evidence of the After Life such as this, from a complete stranger, only fortifies the belief of any medium.

'I'd like to say to you, sir.' the medium went on, 'that mediumship is a vocation. I believe it is *your* vocation. You may be surprised to hear that a book will be written about you and your gift – *and* it will be a bestseller. I want you to remember my words.'

Here she paused and after a moment added, 'I'd just like to repeat that George thanks you profoundly. I'm sure you have done something very special for him.'

I nodded acknowledgement.

'Well with that I say "God bless you" and thank you for speaking to me.'

'Thank you,' I replied.

After the service, Barry and I stood in a corner discussing the messages we had received. We were both amazed at how accurate the medium had been in what she had said. 'Well, at least he came back to thank us,' I said jokingly, referring to George.

'It's funny you didn't get a flat battery, all the times he set your car alarm off,' Barry remarked.

Since my little problem with George, there is something I've discovered about my life and my spiritual journey. All answers to all questions are within me. From my experience of other spirit mediums, I know them to be very self-sufficient individuals. Often, they are aware of things not known by their peers – they possess a sort of archive of knowledge, stored deep within their being. When the need arises, they are able to draw upon this to find answers to apparently insoluble problems.

Slowly, I have become aware of my own personal archive and learnt how to access the information in it. This has given me increased confidence, both in my work and in my life generally. However, I still regard it as very important and necessary to me to have friends and mentors such as Jim, June and Jane who are always willing to help me in my hour of need.

Over the past two years, I have taken part in a number of "Rescue Circles". These exist to help those in spirit and their loved ones in this world in whatever way is necessary. George is a case in point. Rescue work is a very important part of my mediumship. The sense of satisfaction I feel when I am able to help in this way is immense.

In contrast to George, who certainly gave me a headache or two, there was Mr. Collier.

Mr. and Mrs. Collier had been long-standing clients at my salon, until Mrs. Collier had died suddenly of a heart attack and I heard no more from her husband for some months. Then, at the end of a busy morning, I had a phone call and I immediately recognized the voice of the caller as that of Mr. Collier. After an exchange of pleasantries, Mr. Collier explained the reason he had contacted me was because he had heard that I was a medium as well as a hairdresser. His friend had been to one of my demonstrations in Widnes, he said, and had been impressed, so now he wanted me to try to contact his wife, May. He had not come to terms with her death. They were a childless couple whose only surviving relatives were in Australia. I sensed his grief as he spoke to me over the phone. There was a note almost of desperation in his voice, so I arranged to visit him at his house.

When I arrived there the following week, I was taken aback by the preponderance of photographs of May lining the walls of the living room. He had turned their home into a sort of shrine to her. After welcoming me, Mr. Collier explained that he had a firm belief in life after death but he could not bear the separation from his wife which death had brought.

I sat before him with my eyes closed for a moment or two, during which I became conscious of May's presence.

'May is here now, with us,' I told him.

'Tell her I love her,' he said quietly.

'She says "I know, you old fool!"'

Tears came into his eyes, but he still managed a knowing smile. May described to me various events in their life together – a trip to Australia when all their luggage was lost, and his buying her a diamond and sapphire ring, which I described in detail to her astonished husband. Then she told me of her concern that her husband was so consumed with grief that he no longer had a social life and was sinking into deep depression. She wanted me to impress upon him that he must pull himself together. I reported what May said, word for word. As he listened, her husband became very emotional.

'I'm letting my wife down, aren't I?' he uttered.

'No, you're letting yourself down,' I told him.

'Go out and enjoy yourself, spend your money, visit your relatives. This is what May wants you to do. She is telling me that she will go with you.'

Almost two years later, I was at a low ebb. I believed I wasn't worthy of being an ambassador for the Spirit World. I felt I wasn't trusting the information I was receiving and was beginning to think I should cease in my attempts to become a medium. I was demonstrating before a large audience in Liverpool. My first link was with a spirit gentleman, who appeared to be in his seventies and gave his name as "Harry". As I opened my mouth to describe Harry to my audience – there was Mr. Collier standing beside him! I blamed my imagination for this vision and carried on with my description of Harry.

The following week at a demonstration in Widnes, the same thing happened again – there was Mr. Collier, placing himself between myself and my first spirit link. As before, I carried on, somewhat puzzled.

Then, a few days later, all became clear after a client in the salon who knew Mr. Collier well, told me that he had died two weeks earlier whilst visiting his relatives in Australia. It is my belief that Mr. Collier came back to see me as he wanted to reaffirm my beliefs. The Spirit World accepts that we are "mere mortals" and that, as such, we find it difficult sometimes to trust ourselves, let alone Divine Intervention. Trust can be a major issue in this field. I know it was for me.

I feel this tale serves as a good example of how those in the Spirit World can help us here on Earth.

Chapter 12

Martin

It had been a tiring day at the salon. The song, *'Tell me why I don't like Mondays'* sprang to mind. The phone had never stopped ringing. Salesman after salesman asked questions such as 'Would I like a water dispenser? Who supplied our cleaning materials?' Someone offered a cheap insurance deal – he rang twice. Additionally, every customer seemed to have long hair. My 10–30 appointment had hair well below her waist, and so did my 11 o'clock one.

I worked all through the day without a lunch break. Two cups of coffee warded off my hunger. By the time five o'clock arrived, my stomach was growling – it must have thought my throat was cut!

Totally exhausted, I left my poor mother to tidy up the salon. She's always on hand when I need her – I think that's what keeps her going.

'You get off,' she said. 'You look shattered.'

'I am,' I replied. 'I've got to meditate. I'm at Wigan tomorrow, demonstrating.'

'That's what's up with you,' she said. 'That bloody voodoo! I've told you where you'll end up lad.'

'Mum, please!' I begged. 'I really don't want to argue.'

I promised to telephone her that evening and left.

Meditating is difficult for me when I am tired. Sometimes I drift off to sleep. Once, I started at 8–00 and woke up at 11–00.

After dinner, I took a shower in the hope that my body would spring back to life. Feeling much better and awake I retired to my study and settled myself down to meditate.

During meditation, I always commune with my guide, Jason. I talk to him and ask him to help me with any problems that I may be experiencing or any situation that might require guidance. Jason usually has an answer. He's like a best friend, a soul mate and, it may surprise the reader to learn, he has a great sense of humour.

I can recall an occasion when Andrea, Barry and I were at a theatre. We were waiting in the foyer. Andrea and I had had a minor quarrel and the atmosphere was tense and chilly.

Out of the blue, Jason and some of my other guides from the Holy Order of St. Francis of Assisi began to do a strange sort of sand dance in time to the background music that was reverberating around the theatre. I couldn't contain myself – I just burst into laughter, getting some very strange looks from other members of the public around us. However, the atmosphere between the three of us instantly became cordial.

During my meditation that night, a young man had joined me. He had short hair around the back and sides of his head and wavy curly hair on top. He was dressed in a dark blue sweatshirt, which looked a couple of sizes too big for him, a pair of jeans and a pair of trainers.

'Hello, who are you?' I asked.

'Martin. I'm Martin,' he replied.

'Okay Martin. Why have you come along? I asked.

'I want to communicate with my mum,' he explained.

'Do I know your mum?' I asked.

'No, but she's coming to your demonstration in Wigan tomorrow evening,' he informed me.

'Can you come back tomorrow then, Martin?'

'No, I want to stay, David,' he said firmly. 'Just in case I can't get through. There's going to be lots of communications tomorrow and I want to be first.'

No matter how I tried, Martin just stayed there in my mind's eye. Nowadays, this situation would not arise since I have gained the knowledge of how to deal with it. At that time, I didn't know what to do.

My meditation came naturally to an end. Martin wasn't going to go away and to be honest, he wasn't doing any harm, it was that just every time I turned my attention to my mind's eye, he was still firmly present, waiting.

I was reminded of a similar happening not long after my father died. There appeared to me one day an image of dad, sitting on a log in a forest. He seemed to be waiting for something. The image became persistent and I was quite disturbed by it until it came no more. I have thought since that it was my father's way of confirming that I was now a medium and we could keep in touch

All through the night I was aware of Martin, though I didn't feel disturbed in any way. During the next day, whenever I turned my attention to my mind's eye, he was still there.

Martin, who made sure David contacted his mum and used 'Polo' as a code word.

'Are you alright, Martin?' I asked.

Yes, I'm fine, was the answer he impressed upon me.

Six o'clock was the time I had ear-marked for my pre-demonstration medi-tation. Usually during meditation, I ask if there is anyone who would like me to pass on messages to their loved ones who will be at that particular night's event. When I did this, Martin just impressed himself upon me... *I'm Martin, I'm first.*

I decided I would just have to trust in Jason and Martin that night.

We arrived at the Bellingham Hotel a little early. I had done two previous evenings of clairvoyance there some months before and I'd enjoyed the welcoming atmosphere the venue had to offer. Barry had arranged our appointment. He is unbelievably organised. Andrea began to sort out the tickets for when the doors opened. I decided to go to the bar to get us some water.

It was 15 minutes before the doors opened and I sat and asked all my guides and loved ones to draw close and help me. I always ask Jason separately because I believe him to be my main guide and inspirer. I changed my focus of attention to my inner vision and Martin was still standing there, waiting patiently, with a smile on his face.

'We're getting closer to take off,' I said to him, but he just smiled.

Andrea in her turn went to the bar to get some orange juice. When she returned, she walked over Barry and me. 'Hey, it's getting full in the bar.'

I always feel bothered when Andrea tells me such things. Believe it or not, before I go on I'm very nervous and apprehensive, but I trust Spirit and I know that Jason will never let me down.

'Guess who's out there David,' she said smiling.

'Who?' I snapped. Andrea could see that I was nervous and that this was the reason for my irritability, so she said in a forgiving voice, 'Liz, who comes to me to have her hair trimmed. Her son, Colin, is with her.'

'What did you say to her?' I asked.

'Nothing. She was with a friend but I'll catch her on the way in and let her know that it's you they are coming to see. I bet she'll be shocked.'

Not wanting to chat to my audience before starting the demonstration, I sat down in a corner of the room and closed my eyes. If there is no dressing room, I tend to do this since it acts as a signal to others that I am in a world of my own and it helps me focus on the task ahead and leave the events of the day behind.

The doors opened and Barry and Andrea took charge. As Liz entered, Andrea stopped her and took her aside while Barry carried on with his door duties.

Liz was surprised to see Andrea. 'What are you doing here?' she wanted to know.

'I'm with David,' Andrea replied.

'Oh, where is he?' asked Liz.

'Over there,' Andrea said. Liz still didn't catch on to the fact that I was the spirit medium that evening.

'My friend and I have come to see this new medium, David Traynor. He's said to be good,' she said. 'I didn't realise you and David were into this sort of thing.'

'Liz. David *is* the spirit medium.'

Liz was aghast. 'David! Oh, I've never known your surname,' she exclaimed. 'I didn't know *he* is a medium. Wait 'til I tell my friend, Linda.'

The audience was seated comfortably. As I opened my eyes, Liz smiled at me. Her son, Colin, sat at the side of her, staring in disbelief. The audience chatted away. I stood up, welcomed them all and introduced myself, Barry and Andrea.

I always ask members of the audience to turn off their mobile phones. I believe they are for messages of another kind and I can be thrown off track if a mobile starts to ring. Nearly every one of them fumbled for a phone to turn off tones ranged from 'Amazing Grace' to 'The X-Files' signature tune.

Some members of an audience are often nervous when they attend events concerned with the "occult". I believe this may be to do with the manner of the portrayal of this type of subject on television. People think that an evening of clairvoyance takes place in the dark and with the participants joining hands, as in a séance. I always joke that if an audience concentrates hard enough, a *Toffee Crisp* will come down from the centre of the ceiling, an idea taken from an advert on television. It's amazing what laughter does. It puts people at their ease, settles them in and lets them know that nothing "spooky" is going to occur. This audience seemed really receptive. They had come along for a good night and the atmosphere was electric.

I could feel the tension in my head as my friends in the World of Spirit got ready to come through to their loved ones. Using my inner vision, again I returned to Martin and asked him if he was ready. He impressed the answer "Yes" upon me. I asked him to give me the names of members of the audience who had come in the hope of contacting him. The names "Tom" and "Simon" came quite forcefully into my head.

'Ladies and gentlemen, I have quite a young man join me. He's got short hair, quite wavy on the top. He's wearing a baggy sweat-shirt and jeans. He tells me his name is Martin. He also tells me that someone in the audience is his mother and she would know the names of Tom and Simon. Does anyone recognise the description of this young man? He appears to be about 20 years of age.'

A young girl sitting next to Colin practically shouted, 'Yes, yes,' and raised her hand. 'I know who you've contacted.'

'Good evening, my friend,' I replied. 'I'll try to get you some more information, but you don't look old enough to be his mother,' I joked.

'This is my mum here,' she gestured. A rather embarrassed lady in her early fifties began to smile nervously. She was sitting by the side of Liz.

'Good evening, my love,' I said. 'You must be Martin's mother.'

'Yes, that's right,' she replied quietly.

'If you just bear with me, I'll ask for some more evidence and proof of his existence for you. Martin is showing me two vehicles colliding. He is making me aware that he crossed the World of Spirit of injuries sustained in a car accident. The other driver lived. He is also making me aware that he has no ill feeling whatsoever towards the other driver.'

Martin's mother took over. 'Yes, that all makes sense,' she said.

'I feel that Tom is a grandfather link. Martin is telling me that he is with Tom in the World of Spirit.'

'Yes, that's correct. Tom is Martin's Grandad and he is in the Spirit World.'

'But he keeps talking about Simon, he wants to thank Simon.'

Martin's sister looked puzzled. 'I can't place Simon,' she said.

'It's as if he wants to thank Simon for something. Okay…, he's telling me about aunty Alice and uncle George being there with him too.'

Martin's mum smiled. 'Yes, they are. Oh I'm glad he's not on his own.'

'Going back to his accident – he must have had severe head injuries, he's drawing my attention to his head,' I said.

'Yes, he did,' said his mother quietly.

'You may take this condition off me now please Martin,' I said. Spirits sometimes impose certain feelings upon mediums so that the medium they are communicating with can understand and describe their condition before they crossed into the World of Spirit.

Edith and Tom, Martin's maternal grandparents.

'I want to talk about Hope Hospital, Salford and a June anniversary,' I said confidently.

Then, 'Simon. I'm still getting the name Simon. I want to pay tribute to Simon.'

'Simon is a family friend who visited the family at Hope Hospital. He worked at Salford Fire Station. He was a great help to me and my daughter when Martin died,' Martin's mum said suddenly.

'Yes,' Martin's sister said. 'Oh my goodness, yes. Simon the fireman.' They both looked aghast.

'I want to give you the name of Brian and a feeling of great sadness surrounding this gentleman on the Earth plane.'

'Yes,' Martin's mum said.

'There is a father link with Brian,' I told them.

'Yes, Martin's dad,' his mother confirmed.

'I feel Brian has never got over Martin's death. Martin is asking you to call your dad, he says he is a little down.'

Martin's sister said, 'Yes, I'll give him a call.'

'I want to give you the name of Joanne,' I said.

'That's me,' Martin's sister said, smiling.

'And Andrew.'

'That's my brother,' Joanne replied.

'I believe, Joanne, you are not happy at work at present. I'm being told to tell you to speak your mind. It isn't Martin telling you that, it is my guide, Jason. He's telling me to tell you to speak out – get it off your chest.'

'Thanks a lot,' Joanne said. 'I understand.'

'Gretna Green will mean something.'

'Yes, it does. I got married there,' Joanne said.

'I feel Martin was there with you, watching.'

A smile came over her face which could have lit the whole world.

'Also, you will understand the name of Carolyn. She's here on the

Earth plane, only a young girl who has just split up from her partner – I believe she is confiding in Gill at work. Just to let you know from the World of Spirit that she will be fine.'

'Thanks,' Joanne said. 'Yes, thanks very much,' Linda joined in, 'we know exactly who you mean and it is all correct.'

'I want to give you March 17th as a birthday in the World of Spirit.'

'That's my mother's birthday,' Linda said.

'And 25th March too,' I urged.

'Yes,' replied, Linda.

'Martin's stepping back now but he wants you to know that he loves you all and to tell Andrew to come along next time even though he is sceptical – but tell him anyway.'

'We will,' said Linda, smiling.

'Yes, we'll tell him,' Joanne agreed.

'So all of you, please note that Martin's fine on the other side and thank you so much for a lovely communication. God bless you.'

Everyone clapped. Martin's mother and sister looked over the moon. I turned my attention to my inner vision. Martin smiled – *Thank you*, he impressed upon me. *No, thank* you *Martin,* I replied.

Barry had been drawing all the time as I spoke to the audience and was communicating messages from the Spirit World. Barry is a Psychic Artist – it is another form of mediumship. He contacts his guides on the other side and they help him to draw the faces of our loved ones. Spirits can also help Barry to draw people still alive as well as those who have crossed over. Often, he will receive additional information about the person whose portrait he has drawn, and he will write this on the back of the drawing. Usually, this extra evidence makes Barry's links indisputable.

Barry doesn't say much during demonstrations, but even so, the evidence he provides of contact with the Spirit World can be over-whelming for the person on the receiving end. Barry popped the portrait into a plastic sleeve so it wouldn't be smudged and then placed it on the edge of the table.

After I had finished my second successful communication, I picked up the picture completed earlier. Barry's drawings usually help me to make a strong and direct communication with the spirit in the World of Spirit. Information flows, adding to the evidence written on the back of the portrait.

I like to keep my demonstrations light-hearted to amuse my audiences. So, lifting up the picture, I started to hum the song, "Always look on the bright side of life". I walked from one side of the room to the other modelling the portrait – it brought the house down. Laughter is so uplifting in a demonstration of this kind.

Then I began to read out what Barry had written on the back. He chipped in, 'Make sure you get that evidence right. You need glasses you do.' This brought more laughter.

What he wrote was as follows:

'Connie; Mary Ann; Mary Jane; October anniversary; July wedding; happy times, long gone, in the sixties; October holidays for the family; recent birthday, a little girl."

Martin's mother practically shouted 'I can take all that, and the picture – that's my dad. It matches a picture I have of him at home.'

I asked her to clarify the information on the back of the picture for the benefit of the audience so they could appreciate the value of psychic art.

She began, 'the name of my grandmother is Mary Ellen. dad died on October 8th. July 1st is my parent's wedding anniversary. In October, my daughter Joanne and son-in-law Colin, went to Florida on holiday. The recent birthday – that's Joanne's 21st on 13th June. It's definitely my father.'

The audience seemed amazed. Psychic art does have that effect on people. Just recently, Barry drew a gentleman from the World of Spirit and when I held up the picture so the audience could see it, a young girl screamed and wouldn't return after the interval. Barry had drawn a portrait of her favourite uncle, who had not long since crossed into the World of Spirit. His evidence had been far too overwhelming for her.

After the event, Linda, Martin's mother, and Liz, our customer, walked over to thank us all. It had been a great night for communication at the Bellingham Hotel. Lots of people had come through for their loved ones in the audience.

We arrived home shattered. I always crave something sweet after I have been working and Andrea always comes up trumps. This time, a fresh jam and cream scone and a hot cup of coffee were very welcome. As I began to munch, Barry looked up, 'David. Eat slowly, you're pigging out!' he said.

'I'm starving,' I replied. Then a voice in my head said *He's posh, David!* I burst out laughing – it was Martin.

'It's Martin,' I said, my mouth filled with scone. 'He thinks you're posh, Barry.'

'Tell him to get lost,' Barry said jokingly.

Martin impressed upon me that Liz would be coming to our shop the very next day for a haircut. He wanted me to ask Liz to tell his mother that he wanted to communicate with her again, if I didn't mind, and could she come along for a private sitting. I told Martin that I didn't mind at all and that I would pass the message on, via Liz, the next day. Martin thanked me and left.

The next day, Liz walked into the salon. Looking at me with a big smile and she exclaimed 'I couldn't believe it last night. You were great and so was Barry. Linda and Joanne were just overjoyed.'

'Well, Martin came to me at home last night and asked me to help him. He wants Linda to come along to a private sitting. He asked me to gain contact with her through you.'

'I'll call her when I get home. She'll be so pleased and absolutely thrilled,' Liz said.

On the way home from the Thursday night service at Chorley, my mobile phone began to ring. I haven't got a hands-free set in the car

Martin's grandfather, Tom, as drawn by Barry Wilson, Psychic Artist, on 29 June,
2004 at the Bellingham Hotel, Wigan during a demonstration.

so I pulled over to the side of the road. I must admit this usually wouldn't have happened but after a near-miss experience with a hawthorn hedge at the corner of a winding road a few weeks before, I decided to give up the rather dangerous habit of answering my mobile phone whilst driving.

'Hi, this is David,' I said.

'Hello, David, this is Linda, Martin's mum. You do remember me, don't you? Liz is my friend, you know, from the Bellingham?'

'I am so glad you called,' I said.

'Sorry it's a little late. I tried to contact you earlier,' she explained.

'I know. I've been at a service. Now, what about Martin wanting to communicate with you?'

'It's marvellous. I can't believe it, David,' she replied. 'I am just so happy. I am amazed he came through so well. Mind you, he has been through before you know.'

'Oh. Has he?' I replied inquisitively.

'Oh yes. But not so clearly as that. Joanne and I were very impressed by how accurate you were in what you said about Tom, my dad, and Martin being with him. I found that very comforting. And when Barry drew him, we were just overjoyed.'

I told her how pleased I was for her and how much satisfaction it gave me to be able to help her.

I arranged an appointment to see Linda and Joanne a week later at my office. I was aware how important this communication was to Linda and I hoped I would be able to fulfil her expectations. I believe that the greatest loss anyone can sustain is the loss of a child.

I can remember putting the phone down after speaking to Linda with a tear in my eye. I said aloud to Martin, 'Be there please.' And I knew he wouldn't let us down.

The following Monday saw the end of another busy day in the shop and we were both expected, as usual, at our weekly musical rehearsals in Wigan. Barry had had high sugar levels all day and just before we set off for the rehearsal he had experienced a 'hypo' – a little too much insulin, I suspect. He decided not to venture out and I could see he was tired and drained. 'I'm having an early night!' he exclaimed as I left for rehearsal. 'I've just had enough.'

My brief experience of living with a diabetes sufferer has taught me how disabling this condition can be. I can only sympathise with anyone who suffers with this awful condition. I hope and pray, every day of my life, that somebody, somewhere will come up with a cure.

The rehearsals proved tiring. At 9–30 I decided I'd had enough and sneaked out, hoping that nobody would miss my dulcet tones.

As I steered my car into the drive of my house, I noted that Barry's bedroom curtains were drawn and the lights out. He'd obviously stuck to his word. Turning the car engine off, I suddenly heard a voice, 'David, David it's me.'

'Who?' I replied looking around. I thought that someone had smuggled themselves into the back of the car.

'Me, Martin,' the voice said.

'Martin? Martin who? Not Martin, Linda's son!' I exclaimed.

'Yes.'

'Bloody hell Martin! I can *hear* you. You're audible!' I said. It takes a lot to make me to swear.

'Listen. I'll be there tomorrow. Okay, David?' he said.

'Great. But now that I've *heard* your voice how will I know it's you? You know ... how will I separate it from my subconscious?' I wanted to know.

'I'll say something particular, David.'

'Such as ...' I prompted.

'Like ... 'Polo', he replied.

'Alright,' Then an idea struck me. I wondered if it was possible for spirits to bargain. I was anxious to develop my clairaudient ability further so I said, 'Martin, if I help you to contact your mother, do you think you might help me to be more clairaudient?'

'But you *are* clairaudient,' he replied.

'Yes, but can you help me make my gift a little stronger?'

'I'll try,' Martin said. 'It's so important for me to be able to communicate with my mother. If she wants to come along to contact me, you *must* say "yes".'

'*I will,*' I promised.

Then I was aware that Martin was no longer there.

A few nights later, after my usual meditation, Barry, Andrea and I sat around the kitchen table, sipping coffee and chatting about the day's events. Barry informed us that his sugar level had become more stable and he felt considerably better. I'd had a bit of a tickly cough and it had worsened with the hairsprays I use in my job.

For some reason, the tickle started up again so I began to hunt for some throat sweets.

'What are you looking for?' Barry wanted to know.

'A throat sweet,' I replied. 'This cough's really irritating me and Martin's mother will be here soon.

'I've got some sweets in my car,' Barry said. He went off to get them.

When he returned, he handed me some sugar-free Polos. I popped one into my mouth and put the rest in my pocket.

The doorbell rang and I knew that it would be Linda so I requested Andrea to put the kettle on. My guests are sometimes nervous, for one reason or another, and a "cuppa" never fails to calm them.

Joanne had come with her mother. 'Come in,' I welcomed them both.

I led them through into the conservatory and offered them a drink.

Linda asked for tea, Joanne didn't want anything to drink.

After they settled in their seats, I was about to start to speak when a voice said 'Polo, sugar-free Polo.'

'Martin?' I said.

'Yes, David,' he said clearly.

I turned to Linda and Joanne, 'Can I ask you both, if I described Martin's voice as being "husky" and "rasping" would you say I'd be correct? Like this ...' I repeated the rhyme 'Eeny, meany, miney, mo' in as near a representation of Martin's voice as I could – though to my own ears it was not a very accurate imitation.

Joanne and Linda looked at each other astonished. Their eyes nearly popped out of their heads. 'Yes. That's his voice,' Joanne affirmed.

'Polos. Did he like Polos?' I asked. I wondered if there was any significance in his having chosen that sweet to identify himself.

'Nothing springs to mind on that one,' Linda said.

Karen was a neighbour when I died, Martin said clearly. I couldn't believe what I was hearing in my head.

'Who was Karen?' I said aloud.

'Karen was a neighbour,' Linda replied.

'Martin has joined me now, Linda,' I said, hoping the communication would continue.

'Martin is showing himself in Adidas trainers, Levi jeans and a baggy sweatshirt.'

'Sounds about right,' Joanne replied confidently.

Tell Joanne to ring my dad, Martin said strongly.

'Joanne. Martin is telling me that you must ring your father.'

'Tell him I will,' Joanne replied.

'I want to talk about Alan from school,' I said.

'Yes, Alan was his best friend,' Linda said.

'Well, Martin wishes to be remembered to him.'

'I'm still in touch with Alan,' Linda answered, 'I'll let him know.'

'Satinwood Close. Martin's talking about dropping somebody off at Satinwood Close.'

'Oh. I'd have to think about that one,' Linda replied.

'Gill, his girlfriend and Ste, and an August connection. Do you understand what I have just said?' I asked hopefully.

'Yes,' said Joanne and Linda together. 'I understand completely,' added Linda.

I was glad they did. Martin had become a little less audible for some reason. I wondered if his energy were low, or mine was diminishing. I didn't really understand because up to this point, he had been so clear. For some reason, Martin seemed to have changed his technique of communication. He wanted me to mention his friend and a still-born child. This information he impressed upon me and I repeated it as I received the message. Linda and Joanne understood completely.

Next, Martin impressed upon me that Joanne and her husband would be building their own house, then starting a family. After giving this message to Joanne as I received it, she told me that her husband was about to start building their new home and that when they moved in they would contemplate starting a family.

Martin then impressed upon me that he thought that Mark "looked like a fat Benny Hill". Joanne and Linda roared with laughter.

'You've been losing weight, Linda,' I said confidently. 'And Rosemary Connelly springs to mind,' I continued.

Martin's granddad, Tom, and his nanna, Edith.

'Yes, yes I have,' said Linda. 'And Rosemary Connelly is correct – hers is the diet I have been following,' she confirmed.

Martin impressed upon me that his energy was getting low. My clairvoyant inner vision of him began to fade. 'Tell my mum I love her", he urged, 'and Joanne. Tell them, please.'

'He says he'll have to leave now Linda,' I said. 'He wants you to know that he loves you both,' I said. A lump came into my throat and I could feel tears forming in my eyes.

'I love you too,' Linda called out.

'Tell my mum, 'bye. Tell Joanne, 'bye,' Martin impressed. 'He says goodbye to you both,' I said.

'Well wasn't that just wonderful?' I said. I was emotionally moved but I remained calm and cool on the exterior.

'David, you have a fantastic gift. It was as if Martin was actually here,' Linda remarked.

'That was brilliant,' Joanne added.

'Now Edie wants to send her love,' I said.

'That's my mum,' Linda replied.

'Oh, she's telling me off… I should have called her "Edith". She tells me she prefers "Edith".'

'She did,' Linda confirmed.

'She's telling me she's taking care of Martin and he's absolutely fine and she's also saying you've nothing to worry about at all.'

'That is great David. It is so comforting to know,' Linda replied.

'I also have Nellie, George and Tom here. All sending their love, Linda.'

'That's amazing,' Linda commented. 'Truly amazing.'

Joanne sat quietly, unable to believe her ears.

'You will understand an October crossing,' I said.

'Yes,' Linda confirmed.

'And a February crossing?'

'Yes,' Linda confirmed.

'And a July anniversary.'

'Yes,' she replied.

'Now Linda. I want you to hold out your hands,' I instructed. As I looked at her hands, my attention was directed to a diamond ring.

'This diamond ring belonged to a lady in the World of Spirit, aunty Esther.'

'Yes,' Linda replied, amazed at what I was saying.

'She's pointed out to me that there's a diamond missing.'

'Yes,' Linda said. 'There is. Just there at the side.' A finger hid the part of the setting where a diamond was missing.

Jason my guide intervened to request me to stop. He declared that I had given quite enough evidence for one night. As I concluded, Linda re-affirmed that it was like having Martin present. Overwhelmed, she hugged me and thanked me profusely, unaware how much pleasure it had given me to put her in touch with her son.

After Linda had gone, Martin returned to me. He impressed upon me that his energy had indeed begun to wane half-way through the reading. He also indicated his happiness with what had been said and was confident that his mother would feel more content in the knowledge that he was well. Finally he impressed, *David, if my mum wants to come along for another reading, will you please do it for her?*

I told him I would indeed. I liked his mother and sister, who had clearly suffered a great loss in their lives.

Why shouldn't I help them? I had been brought up as a Roman Catholic and our childhood experiences have a strong influence on our adult lives. So, although I can no longer believe that I will be sent to hell for what the Catholic Church calls "dabbling in the occult", I have had a mental picture, from time to time, of myself as a poor little spirit medium, precariously balanced on the rim of the firmament, the red and orange flames leaping up ready to receive my old, knackered body. I am sure that if Lucifer is about to give me the final push over the edge that I could talk him out of it – perhaps I could offer him a free cut and blow-dry!

I was preparing myself for another private sitting with Linda and Joanne, Martin's mother and sister. I must admit, I had been very nervous all that day and filled with negatives thoughts.

As the day wore on, my tension increased. However, as I was driving home after work, a familiar voice in my mind said, *Stop worrying, I'll be there tonight – okay David?* It was Martin. I pulled my car over to the side of the road, sat back and breathed a sigh of relief.

I have never yet been let down by a spirit, so I always trust what they tell me. It is inevitable, I suppose, that I should sometimes be beset by doubts, owing to the nature of my work and the fact that human thoughts and emotions can get in the way of my communication with those in spirit.

As I have attempted to foster my spiritual gift, "negativity" has become almost a physical entity. I can actually see it, even touch it. It takes the form of a black fluffy cloud. When, from time to time, I become aware of it I repeat to myself, 'Negativity go away, positivity is here to stay'. This usually dispels negativity. We human beings are amazingly susceptible to its presence and it can certainly interfere drastically with my communication with the World of Spirit.

Martin's family arrived as planned. After the introductions, I asked Martin to join us. Almost immediately, I heard with my inner ear a familiar husky voice, *Hiya David, it's Martin.*

'Martin has joined us now,' I announced. Some people go along to mediums and give nothing away. They hide their thoughts and feelings thinking that we mediums might pick up on them. This is simply not the case.

Accordingly I went on, 'As I'm talking to you, I am receiving more information from Martin. I have asked him to tell me things that only *you* would know and I couldn't possibly have learnt about you from any other source except Martin.'

I turned to Joanne, who had been listening intently to what I said, but had remained silent, waiting patiently for a message for herself. 'Joanne, Martin is talking about Florida," I began.

'We've just come back from there,' she told me.

'He's just mentioned Scotland and Gretna Green.'

'Colin and I were married there', Joanne replied.

'Now Martin is saying you have had a dental problem – but he is laughing.'

Joanne laughed too. 'Yes, I said that it would be too expensive to get my teeth repaired.' Joanne laughed again.

'Now, I want to send love to you all from uncle Joe in Spirit. He used to have chest problems and difficulty in breathing.'

'That's correct,' Linda spoke for the first time.

'Also, Martin tells me you have an uncle John who is here on Earth who is having problems with his hip.'

'That's also correct,' Linda affirmed.

'Your uncle Joe is asking to be remembered to your uncle John.'

'Thank you,' Linda replied.

'Now, Martin is stepping back. He wants you to know that he loves you all."

Neither spoke, they just looked at each other. Linda smiled.

'Can we make another appointment?' she said.

'Of course.'

Martin had gone. 'I'd like to ask our Martin some questions next time,' Linda commented.

I could sense the uplift everyone had received. Comfort can be gained when you communicate with your loved ones in the World of Spirit.

Chapter 13

Debbie

Wednesday, and I had arrived late for work. Josie, my regular nine o'clock customer, was waiting with washed hair. I'm often late for work and I must admit I have some really patient customers. Bursting through the salon door I announced as usual, 'Traffic was terrible, Josie, terrible today.' Josie invariably laughed.

'I'll ask Andrea to put that alarm clock on ten minutes earlier,' she joked.

I hung my coat up in the staff room and picked up my coffee, which Sue always prepares on a Wednesday. Jayne approached me. 'Listen David, do you remember Debbie? You read the Tarot cards for her a while ago. You used Cheryl's cards?'

'Yes, I remember. Nice, smiley Debbie. She comes to have her hair highlighted,' I commented.

'She intends to come into the salon at 11 o'clock to ask you if you will you try to contact her father?' Jane said.

'Thanks for letting me know,' I replied.

Debbie came in as promised, just as my break started. Smiley Debbie wasn't so smiley. She seemed to have the weight of the world on her shoulders. She explained that she had been going through a difficult period in her life and felt that it would give her some comfort to be in touch with her father.

I don't like to use my communication skills in the salon. I don't think it's fair. Neither do I discuss religion or politics. Although I am happy to communicate for everyone who asks me to, as I have developed my gift, I have come to believe that there are appropriate times and places.

I asked Debbie to book an appointment to see me at my office. Rather disappointed, she explained that she would find it difficult to travel there. The staff room was due to be free for the next half hour so I agreed to do it there and then. To this day, I'm not really sure why I did this.

'Come into the staff room,' I said.

Debbie smiled, 'Thanks David.'

At first, my link seemed rather weak. I was getting the odd bit of information, but nothing concrete. I put this down to the surroundings – the hairdriers blasting in the background, the tumble dryer whizzing and, of course, the phone constantly ringing.

I needed something to help me to focus and to help me establish direct connection with the World of Spirit. 'Debbie, have you something of your dad's with you? Anything, a picture, a ring?' I asked.

'No,' Debbie replied. 'I haven't. Oh... wait a minute. I've got the front door key to my mum's house, would that do?'

'Yes, I'll give it a shot,' I replied.

Debbie foraged in her bag and handed me a bunch of keys. Holding them in both of my hands, I closed my eyes and turned my focus to my inner vision. A man sat in an armchair, smiling. I described him to Debbie who confirmed that it was her father. I told her he was smoking.

'He *was* a smoker,' she replied.

I asked him his name but he shook his head. 'He won't give me his name, Debbie,' I said, 'but he is showing me Country and Western records and Slim Whitman LPs – do you understand?'

Debbie laughed, 'That's my dad,' she replied.

Please tell me your name, sir, I asked again, but he continued to shake his head. He impressed upon me the words, *I don't want to tell you my name.*

'He says he doesn't want to give his name Debbie.'

'I wonder why,' Debbie said. 'Shall I tell you it?' she asked.

'No, please don't. I'll see if I can get it out of him,' I replied.

'Debbie, he has impressed on me to say that when you were at home, he could never get you off the sofa and it's a wonder you haven't got square eyes from watching the TV.'

Debbie burst out laughing. 'That's so true. He used to say that,' she replied.

'He's also impressing on me that he wants me to tell you that he is with you at this hard time and he doesn't want you to make a rash decision – think about what you're doing. *Sir, please tell me your name?* I asked him again. He impressed upon me the words, *I was a man's man on Earth, I always went to a barber's shop, situated in Denton's Green. I don't want to give my name out in a ladies' hairdressing salon, if you don't mind David.*

I explained to Debbie why he wouldn't give his name. She confirmed that he did go to a barber's shop in the Green and that he wouldn't like the idea of being in a ladies' hair salon.

'Debbie, he's not the type of man to say that he loves you, but I know from the feelings I get from him that he really does.'

A tear fell from Debbie's eye. 'That's comforting,' she said.

'He's stepping back now Debbie, his energy is getting low, but just know that he is with you always.'

Debbie smiled. I returned her keys. 'Thanks, David. I needed that, I really did,' she said.

'I'm sorry I couldn't get his name for you,' I apologized.

'Should I tell you his name?' she asked.

'No. Just in case he comes back. You never know.'

'Right, I won't,' she said. She gave me a big hug.

Time was creeping on. As Debbie was leaving, my mother entered the staff room. 'Hello love,' she said to Debbie.

Then Sue came in. 'Did you get your message from your dad, Debbie?'

'Yes, it was great, Sue. Just what I was hoping for,' Debbie told her.

'See, I told you. I told you it would be great with our David,' Sue said.

Mum looked but said nothing. That was a first, I must admit.

'Do you want a coffee David?' Sue said.

'No, we're going into Manchester for a bit of lunch, aren't we mum?'

'We are,' mum replied coolly.

'And we're going to look for a new coat aren't we, mother?' I said, trying to change the subject. Mum totally ignored me. Turning to Sue, she asked whether supplies of shampoo and conditioner were running low.

I think this was her way of saying 'this is a hairdressing salon David, not a Tarot booth' and I knew she wasn't happy about my session with Debbie who was the first ever person I had "read" for months before.

I take my mother out twice a week in the car for lunch and shopping and so we set off for Manchester. Mum seems to use these car journeys as a good opportunity for conversation. Usually, she is up-to-date with national and international news and local events like changes of staff at our wholesaler suppliers' premises in Warrington. I must confess, I don't always listen with close attention to everything mother says. Some of it is of little interest to me.

On this occasion, as my car sped along the East Lancs Road, my mind was on other things so I paid little heed to the one-way conversation – until I was brought back to this world by a voice in my head exclaiming urgently,

David, watch out!

I snapped out of my daydream immediately and braked hard in time to stop the car from being wedged under the back of an articulated lorry. I looked across at my mum and saw that her bottom set of teeth had shot out and now lay in her lap. She snatched them up quickly and replaced them in her mouth.

'I'm a nervous wreck in a car with you driving, David!' she yelled, 'You don't concentrate, your mind wanders!'

I told her I was sorry.

'Sorry? You *will* be, my lad!' was her fierce reply.

'I'll be shovelling you up off the road one day,' she growled.

'Mum, please, I've apologised – now give it a rest.'

Gradually, her anger began to subside and the journey continued at a more sedate pace as I gathered myself together.

Suddenly, from nowhere, a voice came into my head. *It's Ken, I'm Debbie's father, I hope you're both alright.*

It was you who saved us, wasn't it Ken? I addressed the voice in my head. There was no reply, but I knew that he had. *Thanks Ken,* I said still using my mental voice.

I couldn't wait to tell Debbie that I now knew her father's name. My mother's voice, still shrill and angry, broke into my thoughts.

'Mum, I just have to pull over for a moment, I need to make a phone call,' I said. I jumped out of the car with my mobile phone, leaving her searching her handbag for a mint.

'Hi Jayne, it's David.'

'Listen, can you tell me if Debbie's dad's name was "Ken"?' I asked.

Jayne didn't know. She explained that Debbie was a relatively new customer, so she hadn't said much about herself, in the shop.

'Could you ask her if her father was named Ken, and let me know'? I said.

'I will do. She's coming in later to have her hair done, I'll ask her then.'

I turned the phone off and returned to the car. Mum looked at me.

'I don't know how you missed that lorry,' she said. 'I really don't.'

'Mum, I do,' I replied smugly. 'I've got friends in high places,' She chose to ignore this remark.

A week passed and I still hadn't heard from Jayne and assumed that either the name was incorrect or that Jayne had forgotten to ask

Debbie. The following Wednesday morning, I entered the salon late as usual.

'Morning, Josie, traffic's bad.'

Josie laughed and continued her conversation with the lady sitting next to her.

I walked over to Jayne. 'Did you find out whether the name was correct, you know, "Ken"?' I asked.

She looked apologetic. 'No, I forgot David, sorry,' she replied. 'But Debbie will be in again this morning, you can ask her yourself,' she added.

Debbie's dad, Ken, who wouldn't give his name, but saved David from a car crash.

Shortly after this, Debbie walked in.

'Hi,' she said smiling.

Jayne immediately turned off her dryer and said 'Debbie, what was your dad's name?'

Debbie looked at me and smiled. 'Ken, his name was Ken.' Jayne looked surprised. Debbie winked at me knowingly...

Chapter 14

Margaret and Joanne

My friend Barry had been a Quantity Surveyor since the age of 17 and by the time he was 34, he had begun to lose interest in the career he had once found so worthwhile. There had been major changes in the nature of his work which he was not well-disposed to. These changes had not settled well with him. I watched him grow more and more despondent. Sometimes, he came to the salon and watched me cutting hair. He talked to the staff and the customers and was happy to make the tea and coffee.

Traditionally at Easter, the salon is very, very busy and on the Friday evening before Easter last year, I looked at the appointments' page for the following day and realised that with staff on holiday and one member sick we were not going to be able to cope. After some moments, an idea formed in my mind. I devised a little "sob story" and rang Barry. Skirting around the facts, I outlined our difficulties, knowing full well what Barry's reaction would be likely to be. I was not wrong.

'David, ask me to work tomorrow," he said. 'Go on, ask me,' he repeated.

'Barry, bestest mate in the whole of the world, will you work at the salon tomorrow?' I said.

'Yes,' he replied and I was saved.

From that Saturday onwards, Barry worked each Saturday for a considerable time. Then, he decided to give up his job and train as a hairdresser himself. At first, I wondered if this was a wise move but Barry began to demonstrate a natural aptitude for hairdressing and, in no time at all, he had customers booking appointments with him to have their hair coloured.

A lovely lady called Margaret came to Barry to have her hair coloured on a regular basis, as did her daughter, Joanne, who was soon to be married. Joanne looked forward to the big day.

Just before the wedding, she and her mother visited Barry for their usual six-weekly root retouch. Margaret was concerned about her husband who had been having blackouts. Joanne explained that her father had a suspected heart problem and, with the wedding around the corner, she hoped he would be strong enough to walk her down the aisle. Margaret added that she and her husband were planning to spend a month with their friends in Wales, something they had been in the habit of doing for many years.

The wedding was apparently a great success. One of our regular customers commented that Joanne looked like a film star or even a glamourous model.

Weeks passed, Joanne and Margaret hadn't been in touch. Then, one evening at about 5:30, Joanne put her head around the front door of the salon.

'Dave, Dave,' she called out. I noticed her reflected in the mirror and walked over to her. She remained outside the door. Her eyes were red from shedding tears and she looked dreadful. 'Dave, my mother's dead!' she exclaimed.

I stared in disbelief.

'I'm so sorry,' I exclaimed, hugging Joanne as she cried. When she had calmed down a little, she began to explain that her father had had a minor operation on his heart which had caused her mother a great deal of anxiety. Her father had withstood the operation well and had been fine when he returned from the operating theatre. Joanne, her sister and older brother had rushed over to tell their mother, only to find her slumped over the bed. She had had a heart attack – the worry about her husband had apparently been too much for her.

Once their father was out of danger they broke the news to him. His grief was immense and I believe that to this day he has not recovered. We did not see Joanne for a long time after Margaret's death.

One Monday evening I settled down to meditate because the following evening I was to undertake a very big demonstration at Fleetwood, near Blackpool. My meditation took the usual form: first, I prayed for peace on Earth, then for healing for all who needed it and finished with the Lord's Prayer.

As I was concluding my preliminary prayers, my attention was drawn to my inner vision. Margaret, Joanne's mother stood there as large as life.

'Hello Margaret,' I said out loud. 'What are you doing here? Are you alright?'

Yes, I'm fine, she impressed. *I want to speak to my family, Dave.*

'Joanne hasn't set foot in the salon since you crossed over Margaret,' I told her.

No, Dave. She doesn't feel comfortable going to the salon. It brings back so many memories and it makes her sad. She knew how much I enjoyed going there and how pleased I used to be with the way you and Barry styled my hair. She hasn't been anywhere else, Dave.

'We have missed your coming in,' I said out loud.

I've missed it, too, she replied. *I want to communicate with my family*, she added, more urgently.

I paused for a moment, before stating, 'But your family are strong Catholics, Margaret. In my experience, Catholics won't usually have anything to do with spiritualism.'

Again and again, Margaret insisted that she wanted to contact her daughter.

'Well, Margaret, if *you* can get Joanne to walk into my salon to have her hair done, *I'll* tell her you want to contact her. I'll ask her to tell her brother and her sister and I'll even invite them to my house so you can communicate with them.'

Margaret seemed overjoyed. *Joanne will definitely come to have her hair done next week*, she impressed, smiling, and began to fade from my sight.

After my meditation, I explained excitedly to Andrea and Barry what had occurred and what my visitor had promised.

Margaret kept her word and, the following week, Joanne walked into my salon. 'Dave, can you dry cut my hair?' she wanted to know. 'I've not been able to face coming in since my mother died but maybe it's time to move on.'

I was shaking as I told her to have a seat and that I would be back in a moment. I went into the staff room where Andrea noticed the shock on my face.

'David, are you alright?' she asked.

'A bit shaken,' I replied.

'Well, you have to keep your promise to Margaret,' Andrea said.

'I'm very shocked, Andrea, I'm not sure how Joanne will react when I tell her about her mother's wish to get in touch with her family.'

Andrea replied briskly. 'Go and get it over with.'

I asked Joanne to change her chair for one in a corner position where we were unlikely to be overheard by other customers. 'I've got something to tell you,' I said.

'What's that?' she wanted to know.

'Your mother has contacted me, she wants to communicate with you, and your brother and sister.'

'Oh!' Joanne exclaimed. 'I spoke to her the other night in my prayers. I told her how much I miss her and that I wished she would contact me through you. I didn't really believe that she *could* communicate with you!'

She went on to say that she had been driving past the salon and all of a sudden had felt an impulse to come in and have her hair cut. She'd decided that it was time to come to terms with everything that had happened. She added that she had missed coming into the shop.

As I trimmed her hair, she was obviously mulling over what had happened. Then she said, 'I'll contact my brother and sister tonight, and then phone you to arrange an appointment.' True to her word, she did just that.

The following Tuesday, she and her older sister, who was also called Margaret, arrived at my house. I answered the door and welcomed them in.

'I'm really nervous,' said Margaret, and she looked it.

'She thinks Mum's going to appear,' Joanne said, smiling.

She told me that her brother would be along shortly.

'Did you tell your father?' I asked.

'Yes,' Joanne rolled her eyes upwards.

'Dad thinks we've gone funny,' Margaret said. 'He fails to see how anyone, let alone a *hairdresser*, can speak to Mum.'

'I think it's his religious belief and his age that lead him to that opinion,' I answered.

Margaret was on a roll. She suddenly asked, 'David, where is my mum. I always wanted her to be with Jesus and all the angels and saints. Are you saying she's not there?' She was clearly very concerned as she asked this question.

'No, I'm not saying that. Your mother is in the realm of Spirit and yes, there are angels around her and what's more, she is very happy,' I replied.

'It's hard to understand. I've always been led to believe one thing and now I'm hearing another.' Margaret seemed confused and concerned still.

At this point the doorbell rang. 'That'll be Ian,' Joanne said.

I opened the door and invited him in. Ian also looked terrified but after a few minutes he began to settle. He explained that he had long since abandoned his childhood belief in Catholicism. He seemed quite knowledgeable about the various different world religions and beliefs and he told me that he thought there was "something in"

Spiritualism. I found what he had to say fascinating and could have listened to him all night.

Suddenly, Margaret broke in, 'I feel very shaky.'

'Don't be daft,' Ian said laughing.

'It's just because I don't know what to expect,' she admitted.

'Well, if you are all sitting comfortably, then I'll begin,' I said in an attempt to ease the tension.

I turned my attention to my inner vision where Margaret was smiling and greeting me.

'Your mother is here now,' I said. Young Margaret's face reflected apprehension and amazement.

'Where is she?' she said, looking around.

'She's talking to me,' I answered.

'What's she saying?'

'She's worried about her brother, Arthur. He's having trouble with his legs and his back. He's in terrible pain and he is going to consult a specialist.'

'That's correct,' Margaret replied.

'She's also concerned about Roy. I believe he's your husband Margaret. He's been having bad indigestion. When he lies down at night, his condition worsens. Your mother say he's been buying indigestion remedies from the chemist.'

'Yes, that is so,' Margaret replied again.

'Your mother is saying he's very, very stressed and it's to do with his work. He's been studying for exams.'

'This is all true,' Margaret said.

'She wants you to know that she is anxious about Roy, about the danger of him burning himself out.'

Margaret just looked at me. 'My mum *would* say that!' she exclaimed.

I glanced at Joanne and her brother.

'Your mother wants you all to know that she's worried about your father. He's been crying a lot. He obviously blames himself for what happened to your mother. She wants you to tell him that he must stop blaming himself. She says it was as much of a shock for her as for her husband. One minute she was here on Earth and the next she had crossed over to the other side. But, she wants you all to know that she's very, very happy there. Now, I can see a gentleman standing at her side. He's a sort of father figure but yet I don't feel this is your mother's father. I feel that she would have been very close to this gentleman when she was a little girl.'

'I know who that could be,' Margaret suddenly said,

'I am being told that his name is "William", "Bill".'

'Yes, that's who I was thinking of. Can you see my mum now?' Margaret asked.

'Yes,' I replied.

'What does she look like?' Margaret enquired.

'Like your mum,' I replied jokingly. Everyone burst out laughing. I felt the atmosphere finally lighten.

'She's wearing a navy blue, elasticated skirt. I think you ladies refer to it as three-quarter length. It was bought from Marks and Spencer's your mother says,' I told them confidently.

'We buried her in that skirt,' Joanne put in quietly.

'She's telling me now that she likes "the kitchen cupboard doors" but I can't quite understand the other part of her sentence. Has some-one just had a new fitted kitchen?' I asked.

'I have,' said Margaret.

'Well she approves of it – especially the cupboard doors!' I added.

'Has she been around looking at my kitchen?' Margaret wanted to know.

'Yes, she's been watching over you, Margaret.'

'That's lovely,' Margaret smiled.

'She keeps talking about a ring. Someone has "the wrong ring". I don't understand why she is saying that.'

[At the time, I *didn't* understand. Subsequently, I learnt that someone was indeed wearing the wrong ring but did not want to admit this. There are some situations that people deem private, even when it involves someone they love in the after world. I can understand this.]

'Now, your mum is telling me, Margaret, that you have been talking to her photograph in the last few days.'

Margaret admitted that she had.

'And she wants you to know that she heard what you said.'

'She has been joined by a little angel. A little boy. Perhaps he was miscarried before he was born.'

'Yes, I miscarried a little boy, David,' Margaret's face clouded.

'Well, he's still at the side of your mum. She sends her love to you all and wants to tell you to look after your father and let him know that she's watching over him. I'll leave your mum's love with you all. Thank you.' Then the figures disappeared from my inner vision.

Margaret returned to me briefly. She thanked me for everything. As she left I could hear the song *Moon River* being played in my head. A lovely sense of peace came over me. Maybe I'd just spoken to an angel.

Chapter 15

Garry, Julie and Mike

Our house was in need of some renovation. This is to be expected with so old a building. We had tried in vain to get a builder to work on it. Builders who were recommended to us just didn't turn up.

One day, I was cutting the hair of a customer called Garry. As part of the general conversation, I told him about our problem, expressing exasperation that on the previous evening we had been let down by yet another builder. As I spoke, a smile came across his face which I could see, clearly reflected in the mirror. Shortly after, the reason for the smile was explained. Garry had been a builder in the past and disenchantment with his present occupation had caused him to give some thought to returning to the building trade. A good haircut and some gentle persuading on my part resulted in my exacting a promise from him that he would come and exercise his building skills on our home. True to his word, a few weeks later, he had packed in his job at a local warehouse and was on-site at the house. One afternoon, I returned from work early. Garry was in the conservatory talking to the tiler.

'How are you getting on?' I asked, entering the conservatory.

'Slates are a bummer to lay,' Alan replied.

'Well you've made a good job,' I said smiling.

'*I've* just said that,' Garry added.

I went into my office to put away some files. Immediately, I could sense that someone had been in there. I went back to the conservatory. 'Garry has someone been in the office?' I asked.

'I took Dave, the joiner, in to show him my attempt at laying a parquet floor,' Garry said. Garry had done a brilliant job of our floor, the materials for which had been donated to me by a good friend.

Garry looked puzzled.

'How did you know, we only stepped in briefly to take a look and then stepped out again?' he said.

'I could just sense it,' I replied smiling.

'You could *sense* it?' Garry laughed.

'Yes, I'm sensitive you see. I always have been.'

'Go on!' he replied.

'Garry, I'm a medium. I speak to the dead so I have to be sensitive.'

'No way!' Garry laughed even louder.

'Yes I am,' I said.

'That's rubbish. You can speak to the dead? I don't believe it.'

'I can. I'll tell you what, to convince you, I'll ask my guides to tell me something about your circumstances.'

'I believe in what he says,' put in Alan, the tiler.

'Come and sit in the kitchen a moment, Garry' I said.

The smile disappeared from his face.

'What are you going to do to me?' he asked, suspiciously.

'Nothing,' I said.

I gave Garry some names and situations, then some anniversaries, all of which he confirmed were absolutely correct.

Garry seemed shocked. In the space of 30 minutes, his belief in the After Life and mediumship had changed completely. I told Garry I was doing a demonstration at a local club and if he was interested, he could give me a call and I'd reserve some tickets for him. He still seemed unsure and did not accept my offer directly but "played safe" by saying that his wife would probably telephone me. He explained that she was very interested in what he called "Psychics" and had often expressed a wish to contact her father who had died young. I knew that Garry had been greatly surprised by my revelations from the Spirit World and although I was desperate for the work on my house to be completed, I suggested he call it a day and go home.

Afterwards, I sat in the living room, sipping coffee and looking over some leaflets from my local hairdressing wholesalers. Suddenly, my attention was drawn to the far wall of the room. A spirit gentleman was plainly materializing there. He was supported by two crutches and had on a grey jumper.

'Who are you?' I asked aloud.

I want to contact someone who will be going to one of your demonstrations, he impressed.

'Who?' I asked. Even as I spoke, I sensed his unwillingness to give me this information.

'Can you tell me your name?'

No, he impressed.

'Can you tell me your illness before you crossed?' I asked.

Bowel cancer, he impressed.

The man had imaged himself as if he were on a projector screen. He turned and, fading, began to walk away. I found this very strange as I was unaccustomed to spirits appearing and disappearing in this manner. Still, it was no more odd than our ice cream scoop moving from one work surface to another on the other side of the room. Strangely though, when this occurred Andrea, Barry and I, who were having a meal at the time, merely stopped eating for a moment, stared at the floating ice-cream scoop, then at each other, and carried on eating as if nothing had happened.

My mobile phone began to ring. 'Hi,' I said.

'Hello, I'm Julie,' said a voice at the other end of the line. The words were hardly out of her mouth when I was drawn to look at the far wall where the man on crutches was starting to materialize again.

'David, Garry told me about your mediumship demonstration. I'd like to order some tickets,' she went on.

'Julie, may I ask you something?' I said.

'Yes.' There was a note of puzzlement in her voice.

'Garry says you've always wanted to contact your father.'

'Yes'.

'Well, I don't want to shock you by what I am going to say but at this moment, a man from the Spirit World is here with me. I think it may be your father. Will you let me describe him to you?'

'Yes,' she replied quietly.

'He's wearing a grey jumper and he's on crutches …' I began.

'David,' she interrupted, 'You don't need to go any further. My dad was on crutches before he died.'

'Did he have bowel cancer?' I asked.

'He did, and we buried him in his favourite grey jumper.'

'He's smiling Julie,' I said.

'I can't believe that. I must tell our Michael and my mum.' The words came out in a rush. 'I'll ring them now. Thank you, David.'

As I said goodbye, I watched the spirit gentleman fade once more.

The demonstration at the local club was a huge success. Many in the audience had received evidence and proof of survival after death. At this meeting, I told everyone about Julie and when her father appeared on our living room wall. I was drawn to Michael, Julie's brother who sat with her at the demonstration. Although I had never met him before, my guide wanted to communicate with him. I told Michael I felt he was "a sensitive" and if he so desired, he too could nurture his psychic gifts and eventually do what I did – communicate with those in the Spirit World. I also told him he'd been out the Friday before and queued in a local pub restaurant with his wife and two other friends and had complained that the food was "awful". Then I gave him the name of the restaurant and its location. He was amazed and confirmed that all I said was true.

At the end of the evening, Julie, Garry and Michael asked if they could come along for a private sitting. Julie and Mike were desperate to contact their father. I booked them in for the following Wednesday.

Michael and Julie's sitting was here before I knew it. Seated in the conservatory, a nervous brother and sister waited and waited for me to begin. I wondered what was happening myself. It is usual for those in spirit to appear promptly when their relations and friends are waiting for a message from them. All of a sudden, I became aware of a man outside the conservatory, looking in through the window at Julie and Michael.

I turned to them and said confidently, 'We are being watched.' They looked at each other. I glanced towards the side of the conservatory opposite to where the man had been standing. Great was my surprise to note that the figure had changed sides.

'Hello sir,' I said, but there was no reply.

'Hello sir,' I said again. Still no answer.

'Please speak,' I requested.

The man manifested himself on the sofa. The image was much clearer now and I recognised the man in the grey jumper. I turned to Julie and her brother.

'Your father is here, he's sitting on the sofa – like this.' I demonstrated to them how he was sitting.

'That's my dad,' Mike said at once.

'Yes that's him,' Julie confirmed.

'He tells me he was a very quiet man when he was on Earth and he's unwilling to give me his name.'

'That's him,' Mike said.

'He never gave anything away,' added Julie.

Please sir, give me some evidence of who you are, I begged.

Abruptly, he said, *21 Hall Street, St. Helens.*

I repeated the address to Julie and Mike.

Julie exclaimed, 'It's *210* Hall Street, St. Helens – that's where he lived.'

I was pleased with this evidence. 'Your father has just mentioned "Pauline and Joe", his next door neighbours when he was alive.'

'Yes they were his neighbours,' Mike confirmed.

'And Fred, who also was one of your dad's neighbours,' I said, 'and was always standing at his front door,' I added.

'That's correct,' Mike confirmed again.

Their father began to image signposts for Blackpool and Rhyl, both locations Julie said their father had taken them on day trips as children. The evidence was flowing but the spirit gentleman still exhibited a marked reluctance to give his name. I had requested that Julie bring along her dad's watch, the cap he wore at work, and some photos of him. Julie said she asked her mother for these items and her mother was somewhat bemused to find them all together in the top drawer of a tallboy in her bedroom. She was quite unable to explain this and remarked that it was almost as if her husband had assembled them ready for Julie and Mike to bring along to me. In Julie's words, 'this had totally freaked Mum out'.

I took the cap and put it on my head. This action provoked a strong reaction from her spirit father. *Take my cap off you! Get it off your head it's mine!* he shouted.

Take it off, he impressed again. Not wanting to make him annoyed, I did as he asked.

Why won't you give me your name? I queried.

I did something which I'm sorry for.

What did you do?

I met someone else. Her name was Susan.

I left Annette, my wife, for her. It devastated my children. I repeated all he had told me to Mike and Julie.

I could see her sadness. I had no need for the confirmation. I wished this had never happened. The spirit went on, *It was all a big mistake. I loved her mum,* and again I repeated to Michael and Julie what he had said.

Their faces lit up. 'That's what we needed to know,' Michael said smiling.

'And he still loved my mum,' Julie mused thoughfully.

'Well, that's what he's saying,' I replied. 'He regrets everything.'

'He says your mother has met someone called "John".'

'Yes,' Julie said.

'John has been very ill in hospital.'

'He has,' Julie confirmed.

'Well your dad wants you to know that he's been watching over your mum and her relationship with John.' I paused, "listening" attentively to the spirit. Then I turned to Mike. Your father tells me that you have had an interview for promotion in your work but that you are unsure whether you would take the position if it were offered to you.'

'There has apparently been a sacking for dishonesty. You have been upset by the whole thing and you actually regret applying for the job.'

There was absolute amazement on Mike's face and he seemed to be unable to do more than nod his head in agreement.

'You are going on holiday to Tenerife,' I went on. 'I want you to take care.'

'We've just booked it,' Mike said.

'Good,' I replied. 'Apparently, your mother also is going to

Tenerife with her friends. Your father wants her to be careful where she walks, just in case she has an accident. Now your father is stepping back. I don't think he is the kind of man to say he loves you but again, I feel he really does love you both and your mother too. Sir, what's your name?' I asked out loud.

Fred, he answered, so I relayed this to his children and, to my amazement, they began to laugh. 'Why are you laughing I queried? Julie explained that their dad had always said he was "Fred" when asked his name when they were children, but it

Francis Raymond Smethurst.

was just his joke. After a few more requests from me and being given the same joke answer suddenly their father relented and clearly replied, *Raymond. Francis Raymond.*

'Francis Raymond!' Julie and Michael both echoed, looking absolutely astounded. Apparently, very few people knew his full name including Garry and Paula, Mike's wife. To them he was always known simply as "Ray".

As a postscript, some months later, I was told that Michael and Julie's mother had fallen in Tenerife and, as a result of the fall, she had needed hip replacement surgery. With evidence as strong as this, who could doubt that there is life after death?

Chapter 16

Angela and Shirley

We were having a very special guest coming to stay with us for a few days. It was our friend Shirley. We've known Shirley for so long that we regard her as part of our family. I first met her through a mutual friend when I was 17.

This weekend was going to be a sad time. We all knew that. Shirley's identical twin, Angela, had died tragically at the age of 33 on Good Friday earlier that year. Angela had been married only a short while when it was discovered that she had a rare type of aggresive cancer. You can imagine our shock and astonishment when we were told. Immediately, Andrea and I travelled to see her. Andrea couldn't rest until we'd done so. Angela seemed her usual self. She was looking beyond the operation to getting on with her married life with her husband, Tim, whom she adored.

We had Sunday lunch in a local pub, then said our goodbyes. Here was a girl who had been a real friend to me. In fact, she was just like a sister. As she stood in front of me, I didn't know whether I would see her again in this life. Giving me a big hug and a kiss she whispered in my ear, 'Thanks for always making me laugh, I'll always love you for that.'

'I love you too, Angela,' I replied.

We parted and began the tedious journey back home to St. Helens. During the journey, no one said a word. We were all too distressed. The operation, I was told, had been deemed a success but I was beset by doubts. The surgeons had not been able to remove all the tumour, so Angela was given radiotherapy. She had also been experiencing seizures due to the nature of her operation. For a short time, she began to rally. Then, one night, we received a telephone call from Shirley. The cancer had returned and there was nothing more that could be done for Angela. Our grief was immense. The only time I'd ever experienced anything so intense was at the death, eight years previously, of my sister-in-law, Joyce, from kidney cancer at the age of 37 years. She had left four children, my lovely, lovely nieces and nephews. A few weeks later, Shirley rang again to let us know that she and Angela were having a birthday celebration in a local pub on Padworth Common, Berkshire. She warned us that we must expect to find Angela in a very poorly condition. Shortly after we arrived at the party, Angela was pushed into the room in a wheelchair by her mother-in-law. She was almost unrecognizable as the attractive, vivacious girl I knew. I forced myself to greet her, putting on as brave a face as I could. Then, at the earliest opportunity, I found an exit from the room and took myself off into a corridor where I could give vent to my grief by sobbing. It was several minutes before I could trust myself to re-enter the big room. During the evening, Angela held a

Angela, Shirley's twin sister, who died tragically at the age of 33. Her sister was a sceptic until Angela came through with proof of the After Life.

karaoke microphone and sang and recorded her version of *Somewhere over the Rainbow*. She intended copies to be sold to raise money for Cancer Research. Following the recording, Angela was clearly in great pain and her family decided it would be best for her to be taken home. I went over to her to say goodbye and, unthinkingly, attempted to give her the accustomed hug. This caused her to cry out in pain, 'Don't! Don't hug me hard!' I was immediately filled with remorse at my thoughtlessness. However, I do not think that Angela recognised me.

Shortly after this harrowing occasion, Angela died in her sleep, holding onto the hand of her devoted husband.

Unaccountably, at the time we received notification of her death, our house alarm began to ring. It went on and on, with no sign of stopping, until I crawled under the stairs and pulled out the fuse.

That Friday night when I got home from work, Shirley had arrived. The kettle was on and she was sitting quietly in the lounge. We talked for a while, then I explained that Jane, my psychic friend, was picking me up in her car and we were going to our Development Circle in Preston which would give Shirley and Andrea time to talk. Shirley nodded. I could hear Jane pipping her car horn outside.

As I left, Shirley called after me, 'You can give me a reading later.'

'Okay I will,' I replied.

'Oh, I was only joking,' she said. 'I don't really believe in all that sort of stuff.'

The circle ended early that night. Jim was ill and unable to conduct the circle but had left the meeting in the capable hands of Ann, one of the organisers, herself an experienced medium. For some reason, after Ann had announced that Jim was indisposed, the circle became disorganised, the members seeming unable to concentrate. We gathered in small groups, chattering inconsequentially without focus or purpose. A strange, rather gothic member of the circle, whose name I didn't know suddenly announced that she would lead a meditation. Everyone fell silent and a strange atmosphere seemed to envelop the circle. I felt uneasy, almost claustrophobic. I was sitting near to this lady and the feelings that passed through me were indescribable. At the end of the meditation, there was a scream, followed by a loud thud. We all jerked open our eyes. Elaine, a circle member had literally been blown off her chair and landed on the floor in the same position in which she had been sitting. Everyone was totally shocked, unable to move for a moment. Then someone ran over to help Elaine up from the floor. Eileen, one of the longest serving members announced that the meeting should end at this point and expressed her disquiet at what had happened. No one disagreed when the circle was brought to an end. Jane and I left for home. To this day, I cannot give a name to the strange force which propelled Elaine from her chair. I can only believe it was some kind of energy surge.

When we reached my house, I invited Jane to come in.

'There's someone I'd like you to meet,' I told her.

I knew that if anyone could contact Angela for Shirley, it would be Jane. Jane has a wealth of experience. She started out on her spiritual path at a very very early age. I have personal proof of her great ability as a spirit medium on many an occasion when we have been driving home from the Development Circle and she has passed on messages for me from the Spirit World. I just knew that if she met Shirley, she would instantly communicate with Angela and Shirley would be more likely to believe what Jane, a complete stranger, was able to tell her.

'Shirley,' I called up the stairs, 'there's someone here I'd like you to meet.'

Shirley came down, clutching a photograph. 'Hello,' she said.

'This is Jane, my psychic friend.' The two women exchanged friendly smiles.

Then Jane paused only for a moment before asking, 'Have you recently had a bereavement Shirley? I ask this because I feel immense sadness around you.'

'Yes,' Shirley replied.

'There's a gentleman here, in his seventies. Is this gentleman the reason why you're grieving so badly?'

'No, no it's not,' Shirley replied. 'But I might know who that is,' she added.

'I also have a young woman here now and I feel I want to hold my head,' Jane went on.

'Angela, it's Angela!' Shirley broke in. 'It's my sister!'

'Would you understand if I said she had violent pains in her head, a tumour or a head injury, before she passed?'

'Yes, she had a tumour in her nasal cavity and had to have surgery to remove it,' Shirley replied, animatedly.

'Would you understand if I said she was met on the other side by your mother's mother, that is, your grandmother?'

'Yes I would,' Shirley replied.

'Your sister had an operation but the tumour returned and she had a problem with her eye after the operation.'

'Yes,' Shirley answered, 'it's all true.'

Jane smiled sympathetically at Shirley. 'If you could let David have a photograph of your sister, I might be able to form a stronger link with her.'

Shirley held out her hand. 'This is a photograph of Angela.'

Jane took the photo but carefully held it face down. She didn't even see the picture before she described the scene and person depicted. It showed Angela wearing a life-jacket on board a yacht on the open sea.

'This is off the coast of Devon, I believe,' Jane stated.

Shirley was astounded, 'You are absolutely right!'

'My link with Angela is beginning to strengthen. She was only in her thirties when she crossed to the World of Spirit.'

'That's correct,' Shirley asserted.

The tone of Jane's voice changed. 'There's a wedding coming up,' she said.

'That's mine,' Shirley replied.

'You've been making the bridesmaids' dresses yourself and losing your patience with them.'

'That's true,' Shirley said.

'There's a problem with the material, it puckers or frays.'

'It does, it really does,' Shirley agreed.

'Angela is saying if she were here she would make a better job of them, she tells me she was much better at dressmaking.'

'She certainly was,' admitted Shirley.

'She has just told me that she's already been to your wedding.'

Jane looked puzzled, and I certainly was.

Shirley's face turned bright red with embarrassment. Looking first at Andrea and then at me, she confessed, 'I'm already married.'

The look on Andrea's face was one of shock and disappointment. Noticing this, Shirley quickly put in, 'Let me explain.'

Andrea said, 'Well, I think you better had. I was really looking forward to your wedding.'

Shirley included Jane in the explanation. 'David and Andrea are due to fly out with my other friends and family to St. Kitts in the Caribbean this coming April. Mike, my boyfriend (actually my husband now, I suppose) and I are getting married there. Andrea is to be my matron-of-honour.'

'I was looking forward to that,' Andrea said quietly again.

'But Mike, my partner, is American. In order for me to have American residency we had to get married beforehand, here in England, so that everything would be processed for this coming April. Last April was the legal aspect of our wedding. It is this April that we will celebrate our real wedding day with family and friends. In addition, it means that after the marriage in St. Kitts, I can go back and be with Mike permanently in America. I had no choice, but no one knows, no one except the four of us here today.' Shirley was a little emotional.

'Your sister says she likes the wedding dress you are due to wear and she loved your first wedding dress, so I presume you had a special wedding dress here in England.'

'Yes, I did. I had a 'proper' wedding dress.'

'She sends her love to all of you and says you should all take care of yourselves. I'll leave your sister's love with you,' Jane finished.

Shirley was elated by what Jane had said.

I thanked Jane myself. What she had said to Shirley was certainly good evidence of the After Life.

When Jane left, Shirley and Andrea went over and over what she had said. They discussed Shirley's "English" wedding and Andrea remarked that there was nothing else she could have done under the circumstances. Then Shirley looked at me and challenged, 'Come on then, Traynor, let's see what *you* can come up with.'

'Alright!' I retorted, 'just give me ten minutes to open up the Spirit World.'

I always try to quieten myself down before a reading to allow myself to focus and concentrate. Some mediums read "cold" – a type of sitting that has no preparation beforehand. Good communication can be achieved in this way but I like to meditate before venturing to contact the World of Spirit. I went into my office and settled myself down, regulating my breathing pattern – breathing in for a count of six, holding for a count of two and releasing the breath from my mouth for a count of six. Each time I breathed in, I imagined breathing in "plus" signs, to indicate taking in positive energy from the atmosphere and allowing it to permeate my body. Then, as I breathed out through my mouth I imagined exhaling "minus" signs. This signified that I was letting go of all the negativity which had built up inside me. The controlled breathing invariably calms me down and helps me to focus. Next, using my inner vision, I visualise a bright red circle at the base of my spine. I visualise my base chakra, surrounded by beautiful white light. Next, I direct my attention to my sacral chakra which is situated just below my waist. Using my inner vision, I see this as a bright orange circle on which I focus. Again, I surround the sacral chakra with pure white lights. Continuing up the front of my body, I turn my attention to my solar plexus which lies in the centre of my stomach area. I see it as a bright yellow sun. The solar plexus is one of the strongest chakra energy points and when I focus on it, I always feel a sense of power and control. Next, I focus on my heart chakra which I visualize as a jade green circle rotating slowly. As I surround my heart chakra with white light, a sense of love comes over me. Moving up to my throat, I visualise as a light blue circle my throat chakra. [If I've told any lies or had a problem speaking my mind in the previous few days, the blue circle can be covered in dark spots.] After I have enveloped my throat chakra in white light, the spots disappear leaving it gleaming again. Next I turn my attention to the chakra situated in my forehead, between and just above my eyes. This chakra is dark blue. In its centre, I visualize a lighter blue oval shape – my third eye, a window to my clairvoyance. I always ask my third eye to open wide and give me clear sight. At this point I surround my brow chakra with pure white light, letting the light pass through my third eye, illuminating my vision. Finally I move to my crown chakra on the top of my head suffusing it also with white light. It affirms to my spirit guide that everything is alright, that all barriers to perfect communication are removed. A feeling of spiritual uplift comes over me. I'm at one with the universe. I thank my spirit guides for helping me to open myself to their influence. I feel totally positive and illuminated. Next I ask my guides to draw close to me and assist any spirit people who wish to communicate through me. I followed this procedure on this occasion, mentioning Shirley by name.

Then I returned to the sitting room where Shirley was waiting patiently.

'What do I have to do?' she asked.

I told her to sit back and relax but first to take a ring from her finger and let me hold it as it would help me to form a link between her and the Spirit World.

'Does this process have a name?' she wanted to know.

'Yes. It's called 'psychometry'. I'm using the energy which surrounds this piece of jewellery.'

Shirley handed me the ring from her finger. After a moment or two, I was able to give Shirley the name of her grandmother who had joined us from the World of Spirit. Then Shirley's grandfather appeared. Shirley didn't seem convinced at first so I began to describe the interior of her grandparent's house including very detailed descriptions of certain items of furniture. I could see that Shirley was now astonished.

'Your grandmother is telling me that she met Angela when she crossed over, Shirley.' Shirley clearly felt tearful. Andrea gently placed an arm around her shoulders for a moment.

'Go on,' Shirley said quietly.

'Your gran says Angela is fine. She's here with us but she's just watching us all.'

Next I began to talk about Shirley's uncle, a man I had never seen or heard about previously. Shirley was amazed. She confirmed that all the information I gave her was accurate. I returned Shirley's ring.

'I want you to know your family loves you, they've drawn close to you because they know you need their support at this time in your life.'

Shirley thanked me. Then, surprisingly, she asked,

'Do you read Tarot cards?'

'I only have Zen cards. They are similar but they don't have the stigma attached that Tarot cards have.'

We all burst out laughing. Some people believe that Tarot cards are the very essence of evil. My personal view is that much superstitious nonsense surrounds them.

On the rare occasions I have used the Zen cards, I have read them face down, running the palm of my hand over them to allow the different energies from the individual card to guide me as I read. Next, I turn the cards over one-by-one to confirm the statements I have made. I've always looked on the cards as a tool which helps me to connect my higher mind with the all-encompassing knowledge that surrounds us.

Shirley seemed impressed that I knew the identity of each hidden card and that each was confirmed as I turned them over one by one.

I ended with the words, 'Finally, Shirley, just the other night, you and Mike were discussing the pros and cons of having children and, for the moment, you have decided to wait as you are not ready. Can you confirm that you discussed this?'

'Absolutely correct,' Shirley replied.

She added that she was indeed impressed with the evidence I had given her – especially about her grandparents and their home.

'That was spot on,' she said enthusiastically. She gave me a big hug and said goodnight. Then I returned to my office to thank my guides and close myself down.

I find that one of the best ways of closing down is to imagine my guides standing outside my front door and myself thanking them for working with me. I think it's important always to be polite. I say goodbye to them, close my front door and turn the key in the lock, listening to its "click". The door is closed and so am I. Usually it's possible for me to return to watching the TV or reading a book without disturbance from the World of Spirit. I have found from experience that it is advisable to close down, otherwise, if I happen to forget, as I did once or twice in the early days, I begin to feel very drained. The next day, I usually wake up feeling tired and headachey.

It is recommended that those who open themselves to the Spirit World should ensure that they "close down" after any psychic encounter. Failure to do this is likely to result in a psychic "hangover" on the following day.

The next day of Shirley's visit was a Sunday and when I announced my intention to visit the local B&Q Superstore to pick up a few odds and ends, Shirley and Andrea decided to come along for the ride. I don't know what it is about Sundays and DIY Superstores, maybe it's the only day people have time to visit them, but the B&Q car park was full of vehicles when we arrived. If someone had said that half the town had turned up, I could have well believed it. Then Shirley uttered those fateful words, 'I need to buy…'. What followed was a list as long as your arm. Andrea interjected periodically as she compiled her own list. I was beginning to regret inviting my passengers. As I turned the off the car engine, my attention was drawn to my inner vision. There was Angela smiling broadly at me.

Hi, David.

I turned to Shirley. 'Angela has just appeared,' I told her.

'Is it her?' Shirley asked in disbelief.

'Ask her to tell you something to prove it's her,' Shirley said.

All of a sudden in the middle of the B&Q car park, I felt an incontrollable urge to step out of my car, put my arms behind my head and kick my legs up and down. Shirley looked at me, her eyes wide with astonishment.

'That's Ange,' she said laughing.

'Hi, Ange,' she said openly.

Angela showed me a picture of Victoria Wood. I reported this to Shirley, adding 'I don't understand.'

'I do,' replied Shirley. 'We both attended keep-fit classes and the instructress was the image of Victoria Wood, the comedienne. Everyone used to tell her that, and the exercise you were just demonstrating was a routine she taught us.'

'Now Angela's showing me Ruth Maddoc, the actress, who used to be in "Hi-De-Hi". She's impressing upon me the name, "Ruth". Do you understand Shirley?'

'Yes, that was the instructress's name at keep-fit – Ruth.'

Andrea looked amazed.

'Now she's showing me wellies and a padded jacket and she's walking a dog. She is also giving me the name "Judith".'

'That is her dog's name,' Shirley said.

'Angela is making me aware that Judith hasn't eaten properly since her mistress crossed to the World of Spirit. She says Judith looks sad and ill. Her back legs have weakened terribly.'

Some weeks later, Shirley confirmed that all this was correct.

Next, Angela gave me a list of her personal belongings which she wanted Shirley to collect from her brother-in-law's house. She described clothing and jewellery in detail, including a necklace and bracelet bought in Monte Carlo and a set of diamonds which she had given to her mother for safekeeping. Shirley confirmed this.

Finally, Angela asked me to tell Shirley to stop worrying because she was happy and out of pain. She requested Shirley to give her love to her mum, Linda, her brother, David, and her husband, Tim. With that she smiled and left me. A great sense of exhilaration came over me. Shirley and Andrea were tearful. It took us about 20 minutes to compose ourselves before we ventured into the Do-It-Yourself store. Other than 6 *SP2* Duracell batteries, we returned home empty handed.

We may not have returned from the B&Q Superstore with fold-down storage boxes galore, extension leads, or a mixture of 6 small alpines at £4.99, but by the time we reached home, Shirley was joking light-heartedly. This was the Shirley we had not seen for a long time.

That night we were free to dine out at our local Golf Club called Houghwood where the food and service are always excellent. Thus, it is always top of our list for special meals. Shirley's mother and brother, David, were to join us, together with Andrea's parents and my mother. Shirley and Andrea had obviously paid great attention to their appearance. As I looked them over and complimented them, I was drawn to glance at Shirley's wrist.

'That was Angela's bracelet wasn't it?'

'Yes it was,' Shirley replied. 'Can you tell me what else was Angela's?'

I think she was testing me. 'Yes. Your ring.'

'Yes it was! Oh my God David!' she exclaimed.

Then I was aware of Angela's presence.

Have a nice meal tonight, she impressed upon my inner mind.

I told Shirley that her sister had reappeared and what she had said. Smiling, Shirley said aloud, 'Thanks, Ange.'

Angela passed on to me two names, a Christian name and the very unusual surname of a relative on her father's side several generations back.

Shirley was overjoyed. This was a piece of information I could not possibly have plucked out of empty air or made up. Again, Shirley exclaimed her surprise and delight.

From that day, Shirley began the slow process of self-healing.

She returned to my home for brief visits before her wedding on St. Kitts and here I asked Shirley to take up our story.

On returning home from that weekend, I realised I'd been deeply saddened and even mildly depressed since my sister's death but after seeing David and hearing the messages from my sister, I felt as if a heavy weight had been lifted from my shoulders.

The next time I saw David was a weekend in October. I was with my husband, Mike. Now he's a bigger sceptic than I am. We had been out for the evening and had a few drinks, talking and laughing about David being a "psycho". On our return, a slightly inebriated David tried to give Mike some proof of his physic abilities, but the only thing he really came up with was something about eagles. I regarded this as a further proof of David's ability. I had never told him that my husband's favourite American Football Team is the Philadelphia Eagles. I have to say that my husband still believes that either I told David this or that David has some kind of telepathic ability. Some people are hard to convince!

During this same weekend, David told me that a friend of mine, whom he specifically named, would become very ill. Within three months I heard the sad news that this person had cancer.

Well, as my wedding plans progressed towards April, 2004, I didn't have time to see David again until he came to our wedding on the Caribbean island of St. Kitts.

Towards the end of our holiday David was sitting with me and another friend. He continued to describe accurately events in my friend's life that I was aware of but which I know he was not. David then told me that he knew my sister was with me on the day of my wedding. He said he could see her walking down the aisle behind me, like a bridesmaid, which is what she would have done had she still been alive. To provide further evidence in this message he gave me the details of a disagreement I had had with my husband a few months previously. Needless to say, I have had so much proof of David's abilities that I believe he is truly psychic. I would like him to convince my husband.

I now reside in the USA but in September, 2004 I returned home to the UK and stayed with David and his wife. During this visit David gave me only one piece of evidence from the After Life.

It was about my friend who had cancer. David told me that my friend wouldn't live out the year; regrettably I wish David hadn't been right this time, but my friend died in November, 2004. I also went to three of David's spiritual medium meetings in September, two of which were outstanding. The evidence he gave to people, their reactions to it and my questioning of them afterwards, all led me to say that he's one of the best mediums I have ever seen or heard of – on TV or face to face. I would like to believe that David finally recognised his psychic abilities because my sister sought him out of the Spirit World so that she could still communicate with me.

Chapter 17

Janet

I have always tried to count my blessings and have been grateful for the fact that we have had such a successful hair salon when so many find it such a struggle to survive. However, the responsibility for its smooth running is immense and frequently a source of stress to me. A major difficulty is finding good staff – stylists who know what they are doing. There is a national shortage of such people. In the happy event of someone coming along to make an enquiry about employment, I am always ready to create a position if I am satisfied that that person will be "qualified" for the job in every sense of the word. It is not just a matter of expertise in hairdressing. The staff in our salon must also have about them a warmth and friendliness in dealing with our customers.

It was a Thursday evening. I had arrived home from the salon, popped a frozen meal in the microwave and hurried upstairs to get changed for my usual First Night Service at Purple Light in Chorley.

My mobile phone rang downstairs so I rushed to answer it. At the other end of the line, a man's voice, polite and "well-spoken", informed me that he was enquiring on behalf of his wife, Janet, if the "hair-stylist vacancy you advertised in the St. Helens free newspaper" had been filled.

I listened in surprise. I was unaware that I had placed any adverts for hair-stylists in any newspapers in recent weeks. I also thought it odd that it was Janet's husband and not Janet herself who was making the enquiry. However, the thought uppermost in my mind was that I desperately needed another hair-stylist and if Janet were a suitable person, I should want her to start immediately.

So, very politely I said, 'Yes, the position is still available. Is your wife qualified in all aspects of ladies' and gents' hairdressing?'

'Yes she is. She's working at the moment, that's why she hasn't phoned herself.'

'She gave up hairdressing a short while ago to work in a petrol station but she absolutely hates it there and she misses hairdressing. If you wanted to interview her and she was suitable, she could start straight away.'

Jubilantly, I arranged to interview Janet at 5-30pm in the salon on the following day.

For a few moments I continued to puzzle over the fact that I had not placed an advert in the local newspaper.

When Barry walked in at the door, the first words out of my mouth were 'Have you placed an ad. in the free newspaper for a hairstylist?'

'Not to my knowledge,' He grinned.

It transpired that the newspaper *had* printed an advert – one that we had previously placed with them – and the next day they telephoned to apologise and assure us that there would be no charge for the advert. Janet came to the interview and lived up to expectations. She had excellent practical skills and a pleasant personality, as well as having an attractive physical appearance and being smartly dressed. Although she was in her forties, she certainly did not look her age. I was delighted when she agreed to start at the salon the following week.

When she had worked only a couple of days, Andrea remarked that Janet had fitted in perfectly and seemed always to have been at the salon.

That same evening as we were finishing our meal, my attention was directed to my inner vision where I became aware of a boy aged about eleven smiling at me. 'Hello there,' I said. Barry and Andrea broke off their conversation to look curiously at me. Then Barry asked, 'Has somebody joined you?'

'Yes. A young boy,' I replied. I turned my attention back to him, saying aloud 'What's your name?' I had difficulty "hearing" the first part of his reply but caught the word "Michael", which I assumed was his name.

You know my mum, he impressed on me.

I told Andrea what he had said and asked her if she could think of any of our acquaintances who had lost a child. She pondered briefly, then shook her head.

'Were you ill Michael, before you crossed over to the World of Spirit?' I asked him.

'Yes,' he replied, audiently now. 'I had myeloid leukaemia.'

'Oh dear. Where did you cross over? Was it at home or in a hospital?'

'In Alder Hey Hospital,' he replied again, audiently.

I relayed all the information to Andrea as I received it. She continued to look baffled.

Barry said, 'Ask him if he can show you a picture of his mum.'

The boy must have heard Barry, because seconds later he did just that. 'It's Janet!' I said faintly.

'Janet who?' Andrea asked.

'Janet at the shop who has just started to work with us. This must be *her* son, Michael. He is showing me Tasmanian Devil pyjamas with a Marks & Spencers label in them. It says "Size 11-12". Are these your pyjamas, Michael?'

'Yes,' Michael replied audiently.

He repeated the words, 'The 6th July, the 6th July', several times, and then he left. He had been with me for about 20 minutes. 'He's gone now, bless him,' I said. 'Do you think I should say anything about this to Janet?' I asked the others.

James Michael Whittle, who sought out David so he could pass on his love to his mum.

Andrea pointed out that we knew very little about Janet and we certainly didn't know if she had had a son who had died so if I *did* tell her, I would need to broach the subject very carefully.'

Barry thought that any mother in the position of having lost a child would want to know about the child's attempts to communicate.

'I certainly would,' commented Andrea.

'Then I think Janet should be told,' was Barry's opinion. He added that he thought it would also be a good idea to attempt to contact the boy again, in order to gain more information to pass on to Janet as evidence of his continued existence. Barry said that in such a case, where the boy's mother was likely to be comforted and cheered by contact with her son, I should use my gift to the utmost.

On the following Thursday when the salon was unusually quiet, I decided to seize the opportunity to speak to Janet. I called over to her 'Can I have a word with you in private, Jan?'

'I'm not in trouble am I?' she queried anxiously.

'Not at all!'

I did not lower my voice as I said this so the girls took the hint that I wanted to speak to Janet alone and, without fuss, they took themselves off to the staff room to chat and drink coffee. 'Janet', I said gently, 'did you have a son who died – perhaps ten or eleven years old?' Her eyes opened wide with astonishment. 'Was his name "Michael"?' I continued.

'James Michael,' she said calmly. 'He had myeloid leukaemia.'

'He passed over in Alder Hey Hospital, didn't he?'

'How do you know all this? I don't know how you could possibly know. I've never told anybody.'

'I'm a medium, Jan. I can communicate with the Spirit World. Your son came to me whilst I was having my dinner at home one night recently. He imaged to me Tasmanian Devil pyjamas, size 11-12, from Marks & Spencers.'

Jan looked stunned. 'They were his pyjamas and I know where they are,' she replied. I waited anxiously for further reaction from her as I was unsure whether I had done the right thing in telling Janet. I tried to read her thoughts in her face. At last, I said,

'Are you pleased I told you?' Janet became emotional.

'Yes. Of course,' she whispered.

'I've got something else to say, Jan.'

Jan dabbed at her eyes with a tissue. When she seemed calmer, I went on, 'James is here with me now.'

'Oh my God, David,' Jan said, 'I can't believe it.'

'He's saying "Hello, mum". He's telling me he loves you lots.' I waited for her reaction again as she gathered her thoughts. So I asked her permission to ask James to give me some more information about the circumstances of his life which would convince his mother that I was truly in contact with her son.

'He tells me that on the back of his wardrobe door are posters of his favourite football team and his wardrobe is in the garage.'

Janet confirmed this with a nod of her head. She was, naturally, very emotional.

'He said his sister Gemma had painted a picture and it had been placed into a special person's coffin – but he's not telling me whose coffin.'

'It's all true, David.' Janet answered.

'Now he's showing me Alder Hey Hospital and he's making me aware that he left this world from there.'

'He did.' Jan replied. She began to look a little more collected.

'James says you were thinking about him the other night and you became very upset. He was in the house. He wants you to know that he's fine and that he is near you all the time.'

'I sense him near me, David,' Janet said strongly. 'He's always at home. When I am quiet I know he's there.'

'He's talking about football stickers and his headstone in the cemetery.'

'I know what he means,' Janet said. 'Some of his school mates stuck football stickers on his headstone and I left them there, despite the fact that several members of my family disapproved. I saw it as his friends' way of dealing with James' death.'

'James is pleased with them,' I told his mother.

What James told me next made me both sad and angry on his mother's behalf – that Janet had spent a large sum of money in consulting a variety of mediums in an attempt to contact him. 'He says you went to a medium in Southport who charged you £20 and when you came out you told the friend who was with you, "it was a load of rubbish".'

'This is true,' she admitted.

'James says he was with you on that occasion in Southport and he found it amusing.'

Janet smiled, 'Well tell him *I* didn't. It cost me £20.'

James' energy began to wane at this point and his image was less clear to me. I told Janet this and passed on his parting words, 'He's sending his love to you, his dad and his sister, Gemma. He wants you to know that he loves you lots.'

Janet looked up. 'Thanks, David. It's really helped me, it really has.'

Janet seemed keen to tell the rest of the staff about her message from her son and they were pleased for her. She had already become a popular member of the staff in the short time she had been at the salon. She is still with us and I hope she will be for many years to come. None of us will ever forget the night when James came to dinner at our home.

Chapter 18

John and Malcolm

There seems to be a great deal of interest among the general public in the process of mediumship. I am asked many questions, and one question in particular: am I, as a medium, always able to contact a particular individual for a particular person who has come to consult me? My answer to this is that there are no guarantees. It is fairly common for a client to come along for a private sitting in the hope that I will be able to contact a certain loved one for them and a completely different individual will appear.

Here is an instance of this. John had come for a private reading in the hope of communicating with his mother, who had passed over about five years previously. When John booked an appointment with me, he made no mention of whom he wanted to contact.

A very nervous young man in his late thirties sat opposite to me. 'John,' I began, 'do you understand a connection with Salford?'

'Yes,' he asserted.

'I have the name "Billy". Your grandfather from Salford?' I queried.

'That's correct,' he replied.

'He's telling me that you have a lovely little boy and your wife is expecting another child.'

'That's spot on!' John exclaimed.

'He says you have moved into a four bedroomed detached house near Crewe, in Cheshire.'

'This is unbelievable! Really unbelievable, David. All this is true.'

'Billy is talking about your mother, Sheila. "Sheila" is your mother's first name, isn't it?'

'That was her first name.'

'Billy says that your mum has been in the World of Spirit for about five years.'

John seemed greatly affected by the mention of his mother. 'I am shaking,' he confessed.

'Billy wants you to mention himself and Sheila to Pat and Mary.'

'Those are my mother's sisters,' John put in.

'Yes, but they are still here on Earth.' I said.

'Yes,' John answered. 'I'll tell them.'

'Billy's wife Mary is with him. She wants to send her love to you. She is giving me the month "April". Does that mean anything to you?'

Without hesitation, John replied, 'Yes – that's the month in which she died.'

At this point Billy and Mary began to fade, so I reiterated to John that they and his mother, Sheila, all sent their love.

Although obviously pleased at the contact with members of his family, John looked puzzled.

'May I ask you a question, David?' he said at last.

I nodded.

'I came here hoping that you would be able to contact someone else for me. Not my grandfather. Why didn't that person come through for me?' I could sense his disappointment.

'Well, John, you had a choice of whether to come here tonight, or not to come. You chose to come. Those in the Spirit World also have that choice. Sometimes they feel that the time is not right for them to communicate, but they have a choice. I, as a medium, can only communicate with those who present themselves to me. I cannot summon those who do not. Perhaps the person you were hoping to hear from chose not to get in touch because they felt now is not the right time.'

The look of disappointment remained on John's face and he admitted that he had built up his hopes of contacting a certain person.

'But at least with the evidence you have given me, I know there is life after death and so I will see this person again.'

He shook my hand and left. I returned to my conservatory to turn out the lights, feeling a little regretful that John had not been entirely satisfied with his "sitting". Quite suddenly a woman's voice said clearly, 'Hello, David.' As a reflex action, I replied, 'Hello' before realising there was no one in the conservatory.

'I'm Sheila, John's mother,' said the voice, and then went on, 'I stood watching at your conservatory door when John was here just now. I am very proud of him. He has done so well for himself. He started his own business and it has gone from strength to strength. His wife, Joanne, is lovely, and their son Ben is the apple of my eye.'

I knew instinctively that it was his mother that John had wished to hear from. So I asked Sheila why she had not chosen to come through during the sitting. 'I wish you had done so,' I added, 'that's what he came for.'

Sheila made me understand that she had been too nervous to do so, but then requested me to ask John to return.

'Tell him there's ducks over Ben's bed and he will believe you.'

'Couldn't you call him on his phone, now?'

I said I would do so and Sheila left. I took my mobile phone and dialled John's number. His phone was set on answer machine.

'Hi John, it's David. Could you give me a call the second you get this message, I need to speak to you urgently?'

Suddenly a thought came into my head. *He's called at the chip shop; he's had no tea.* 'Thanks,' I said aloud. Within a very short time, John called me back and I told him that as he was leaving my house, his mother appeared in the conservatory.

'Did she?' exclaimed John eagerly.

'She loves you and your wife, Joanne, and little Ben.'

There was a short silence at the other end of the phone. 'I didn't tell you my wife's name or my son's name.' John said slowly.

'Also, John, your mother insisted that I should tell you that there are ducks over Ben's bed. She explained that if I give you this message, you will believe me.'

'I certainly do,' he replied. 'The ducks are on a mobile which my mum bought for me when I was a baby. When Joanne and I moved into our new home, we found it as we were unpacking our belongings. It's a children's mobile with five mallards dangling down from it. We put it over Ben's bed and told him that his nan would be watching over him. That's what my mother was referring to.'

'As a matter of interest John,' I asked then, 'have you just called at a fish and chip shop *en route* from my house?'

'Yes. I've had no tea. How did you know?'

'Your mother told me.'

'How incredible!'

'Your mum wants you to return to my house. She was nervous about coming through earlier but she definitely wants to be in contact with you.'

'When can I return, David?' John asked eagerly.

'Not tonight John, I am just about to have my evening meal but would tomorrow evening suit you?'

'Yes. I play five-a-side football tomorrow. It finishes at 7:30. I'll come after that. Thanks you so much.'

He sounded much happier and I felt happier too. The most worthwhile thing about being a medium is the potential to cheer and comfort those who have lost a loved one.

John returned the following evening. As he settled into his seat in the conservatory in readiness for the sitting, I was aware of his mother standing in the doorway. It was as if she were there to welcome him.

'Hello Sheila,' I said aloud. John's eyes lit up.

'Is my mum here now?' he asked.

I smiled and nodded. From the doorway, Sheila greeted me in a faint but clear voice. After the disappointment of the previous evening, I wanted John to be absolutely certain that I was in touch with his mother. Using my inner voice, I asked Sheila to give me incontrovertible evidence of this. Sheila began by telling me that she had only one son, John, an only child. He confirmed this immediately. She went on to say that she had divorced John's father when she was 40 years old. John said this was so. Her husband's name was Malcolm. It was apparent to me that Sheila had highly-developed spiritual skills. Sometimes audiently and sometimes clairvoyantly, she made her meaning clear to me.

After she had given me the name "Malcolm", she projected an image of a punch bag – the kind used by boxers – and then showed me a tear falling from her eye. With these images came great emotion. I could feel it flooding through my own being. 'Your mother divorced your father because of his violence towards her,' I told John.

'Yes, that's correct David.' John replied quietly.

Next, there came into to my inner mind the clear image of an ashtray filled with cigarette ends. A strong feeling of nervousness came over me. I saw a hospital. Sheila's message was that she had been a chain-smoker and had two nervous breakdowns as a result of her husband's violence. John confirmed this.

The thought came to me that it was perhaps because she had been so frightened by her experiences in life that Sheila had been hesitant to trust me as a medium to communicate with her son on the previous evening. I told John this.

'Yes,' he answered thoughtfully, 'that would make sense. Mum went through hell with my father and she never trusted any man after that.' John's face hardened and I saw his hands clench on the arms of his chair so that his knuckles stood out white. 'I have immense anger and hate towards him. I can never forgive him – ever.'

Suddenly, tears began to well up in his eyes. He brushed them away with a jerky movement of his hand. 'I'm sorry,' he muttered, embarrassed.

'There is no need to be,' I told him. With my inner vision, I could see Sheila quietly waiting for her son to compose himself. Presently, she impressed upon me that *she* had forgiven Malcolm and wanted me to pass this information on to John. She was also anxious that John should forgive his father.

'My mother had so much to put up with from my father when she was alive, I don't understand how she *can* forgive him,' John observed.

At this point, I had the distinct impression that John did not believe what I had just said to him.

'John,' I began, 'those in the World of Spirit are able to look back over their lives from a different angle. It is my belief that your mother has evolved spiritually. She will be aware that if she continues to bear a grudge against your father, her spiritual progress will be halted. She will be able to understand why your father acted as he did and so she can forgive him. What happened in the past is history and cannot be changed. That is why your mother wants you, also, to forgive your father.'

I paused while John appeared to be thinking about his mother's request – or perhaps he was still doubtful whether she had actually made such a request.

Sheila suddenly made me aware that John had bought a new garden shed from a local D-I-Y centre during the previous weekend. It was her way of providing further evidence that what I had told her son was coming from her. After a moment of silence, John said, 'You couldn't possibly have known any of what you have told me from any source but my mother.'

Sheila took this opportunity to reiterate that she wanted John to visit his father who had mellowed with age.

'She wants you to know that age and experience have changed him for the better.'

Then Sheila impressed upon me that John should take his son with him; Malcolm would be very happy to see them both.

'Oh I don't know about *that*, Mum,' John replied, addressing Sheila directly.

An image of a cat appeared before my inner eye and with my inner ear I heard the name "Tabby". I told John this.

'Tabby was my cat when I was a boy. Has she got him there with her?' Sheila nodded. 'Yes she has,' I confirmed.

I could sense that Sheila's energy was beginning to lessen. My heart was filled with love; the feeling was so intense that I knew that she wanted me to tell John how much she loved him.

'John, your mother is leaving us now. She wants you to know that she loves you. She is proud of you and your family.'

'Tell her that I love her too, David,' replied John, with tears still in his eyes.

Sheila acknowledged what John had said.

Some months afterwards I had a telephone call from a well-spoken man whom I imagined was in his late sixties.

'David, I'm Malcolm. My son John came along to see you several months ago. He wanted to contact his mother. She was called Sheila. Do you remember?'

I couldn't at first recollect who Malcolm might be. So many people come to my home for sittings and, in addition, I meet a huge number at mediumship demonstrations.

But the name Sheila brought back into my mind the emotional

sitting I had had with John. 'Yes, I remember now. How can I help you, Malcolm.'

'Well,' he replied, 'I would like to thank you. I heard from John that he had been to see you and you had passed on a message from his mother that she wanted him to contact me. It was many years since he had done so. It came as a great surprise when they knocked on my door – he and his wife and baby Ben. His wife has had another baby boy since then. I've got another grandson,' he said proudly.

I congratulated him. 'You must be very proud,' I commented.

'I am and, what is more, they have called him David Malcolm.'

'That's wonderful,' I replied.

There was a silence at the other end of the telephone for a moment or two. Then Malcolm said in a more subdued tone of voice, 'the reason I've called you, David, is because I am terminally ill myself. I have a tumour on my liver. I would like to come to see you. Would it be possible for you to try to contact Sheila and ask her to meet me when I get to the Other Side?'

'Yes, of course,' I replied.

I told Malcolm I would go and find my diary to write in an appointment. As I put down my phone, my attention was drawn to my inner vision. Sheila stood there, smiling.

I greeted her and in a faint voice she observed, 'He's changed,' then added, 'tell him I'll be there.'

I thought it best to offer Malcolm an early appointment in view of his illness.

'How does Friday sound, Malcolm, at 6.30?'

'Fine David, that sounds great. I look forward to meeting you then.'

Malcolm never made it to his private sitting. He crossed over in the early hours of the next day. When Sheila promised she would be there, I thought she meant she would be there at his private sitting when, in fact, she must have meant at his crossing. I was glad that Malcolm and John had rebuilt their bonds as father and son and that Malcolm had known his daughter-in-law and his two lovely grandsons. It meant a lot to John that his mother had been able to forgive his father and that they were reunited in the World of Spirit.

Chapter 19

The Tarot Card Reader

As I look back over my spiritual development, I recognise that there has come with it a strong sense of personal responsibility. I am merely the *medium* through which messages come from the Spirit World. Shirley mentioned in the account given earlier that I had told her a friend would become seriously ill. Hers is a special case as I regard her as almost a family member and I was willing to answer questions. I would not normally impart such information. I believe that it would be unethical to do so and I would not want to cause distress or anxiety to anyone. Unfortunately, there *are* mediums who are not constrained by ethical considerations. This is to be deplored. I will give an example of the kind of thing I mean.

One Saturday tea-time, I came home from a long hard day in the salon, kicked off my shoes and practically dropped onto the sofa with weariness. Although my work had been tiring, the main reason for my condition was that during the previous night, we had all been awakened from sleep by doors opening and closing, footsteps along our landing and all manner of strange noises downstairs. Sometimes, I wish that those in the Spirit World would ask me for a guided tour of the house instead of having a look around whilst I'm trying to get to sleep! I was beginning to drift off to sleep as I lay on the couch. Suddenly I was aware of my foot vibrating. As I leapt off the couch my mobile phone fell onto the carpet with a soft thud. I had turned off the ring tone earlier and set it onto vibrate mode. Half-asleep, I picked it up and said, 'Hello!'

At the other end of the line, a female voice with a pronounced Liverpool accent enquired hesitantly if I were the spirit medium David Traynor. When I answered in the affirmative, the girl asked for my help.

'I'm heartbroken, I really am. My sister paid a visit to a psychic medium for a Tarot card reading and the fortune teller has told her something awful. She's in a dreadful state and so am I. We've not eaten properly for a week and Carla, my sister, has had to stay off work because she hasn't been sleeping properly.' With that, the lady burst into tears. 'What are we going to do?' she said.

'Come over to see me, love, and we will talk about it.'

I knew that I was in no fit state to talk to anyone but such was the lady's distress that I felt compelled to help her.

She continued to sob down the telephone.

'Come now,' I said, 'Collect your sister if you can.' I gave her my address.

Then, I decided to take a shower to waken myself up a little.

Here is a tip for anyone who has aspirations to become a medium (or for anyone else, for that matter). If you need to be alert and able to spring into action quickly, take a shower. It can remove your negativity and cleanse and re-align your chakras, the energy points throughout your body. After soaping your body, let the water run down your face, neck, trunk, arms and legs and, as you do so, imagine thick brown mud running off your body. With the force of the water, see it run away from your feet; imagine it going down the plug hole. Then repeat the process down your back; feeling the mud flowing away down your back. Imagine the thick brown mud symbolising the negativity that you've generated throughout your day washing away down the plug-hole. Free from negativity, you can now realign your chakra points. Let the water flow onto the crown of your head. Imagine it flowing down through the centre of your body. Feel the water cleansing each chakra. Then rub yourself dry with a towel and you should feel balanced, vibrant, alive and very positive.

Within minutes of my finishing this invigorating ritual, the door-bell rang and I opened the door to two ladies whom I judged to be in their early forties. They were both weeping and were holding tightly onto each other. What had the fortune teller told them that could be so very, very bad? I ushered them in, ascertained that their names were "Linda" and "Carla" and went and put the kettle on.

'Now what's up?' I asked.

Linda looked at Carla, 'You tell him, because I'll get upset.'

Hesitantly at first, and then in a rush of words as if she wanted to get the tale over quickly, this is what Carla told me. She had been going at regular intervals over the past three or four years to a woman she described as a "fortune teller" in the Dock Road area of Liverpool to have her cards read. Twelve months previously, the fortune teller had correctly foretold her father's death from lung cancer within the month. Although very shocked when this information was imparted to them, Carla and her sister, Linda, were aware that their father was close to death, so what they had been told was not entirely unexpected. Besides being upset at the fortune teller's prediction, Linda was very angry and she had made Carla promise never to go near this particular psychic, or any other, ever again.

With my inner eye, I could see my own spirit guide, Jason. He was trying to give me some information.

Very gently, I said to the sisters, 'I believe this fortune teller has told you that your mother is going to cross over before Christmas. Am I correct?'

Even before Carla answered, I could see by the astonished expression on both women's faces that I was.

'Yes, you are,' said Carla.

'For the past three months, our mother has had a cough which has been getting worse and worse. She is very breathless when she walks. The doctor sent her for a chest X-ray last week.'

Linda broke in, bitterly, 'That was the day Carla decided to go to the bloody gypsy!'

'She told me about my mum's chest being bad', went on Carla, 'and the doctor sending her to the hospital for X-rays, but she didn't leave it there. She said my mother has lung cancer and will be dead before Christmas.' 'We love our mum, we don't want her to go,' Linda interrupted again.

'Well firstly girls, everyone will cross over one day, it's an unavoidable fact of life, but when that day will be is in the hands of our Lord …' I began.

'So you don't believe that this fortune teller could actually tell me that our mother is going to die?' asked Carla eagerly.

'I couldn't say that for sure Carla,' I replied. 'All psychics and mediums are different. They all have their own particular way of communicating with you, their client, with their guides and the loved ones on the other side. Some use their intuition and what I call "gut-feelings". Sometimes they "pick up" on the client's body language and the client's reactions to statements they have made. So, for instance, this fortune teller could have said to you, Carla, 'Your mum, is she still alive?' She would have asked you a question.'

'That's exactly what she did say,' Carla replied.

'And your reaction, Carla, would have been, "Oh yes, yes she's still alive?"'

'Yes, I did say that, and… oh! I said she hadn't been well.'

'Then it's likely she made some comment about your mother's health, re-iterating what you had just said.'

'Yes,' muttered Carla faintly.

'Perhaps, she mentioned colds and flu.'

'I'm amazed! This is word for word,' Carla said.

'You probably let drop the information that your mother has a bad chest and it wouldn't have taken the fortune teller very long to put two and two together and mention X-rays.'

Carla looked stunned.

It took a couple of moments for all this to sink in, then Carla exclaimed, 'That's exactly what was said, and then my reply was, "she had them done today".'

Linda exclaimed somewhat scornfully, 'You *told* her! How stupid!' Carla looked shocked, then sheepish.

'Linda's right,' I explained, 'at this point, the fortune teller would have used her imagination and her intuition.'

Linda looked puzzled.

'Carla brought home a tape-recording of her session with the fortune teller. None of what she's just admitted she told the fortune teller appears on the tape. Why?'

'That's a good question, Linda.' We both looked at Carla quizzically and she soon came up with the explanation.

'She paused the tape at frequent intervals.' She said was doing this so she wouldn't run out of tape before the end of the session.'

'I rather think her true reason was that she wanted to 'edit out' what you were giving her in the way of clues so that when you played back the tape, you would only hear her predictions on it.'

'But she *did* say mum was going to die,' insisted Carla.

I replied, 'I think there is little chance of that prediction coming true.'

I looked at Linda. 'What do *you* think, Linda?'

There was relief on Linda's face as she said, 'I'm much less worried now.'

Carla seemed inclined to pursue the subject. 'If psychics work in that way, how do mediums work? Where does *their* information come from?'

I explained that mediums are able to communicate with those in the After Life, usually with the help of spirit guides. The guides are entities who may or may not have walked this earth. As I was in full flow with my explanation, I became aware of Jason manifesting himself and I asked the ladies to excuse me whilst I directed my attention to my inner vision.

Jason presented an elderly lady whom he said was anxious to communicate with Carla and Linda. This lady hobbled into my inner vision. I could clearly see that she was quite tall and had white curly hair. She was wearing a blue dress and white cardigan. I described her in detail to my visitors. Then I paused, waiting to receive information from the elderly lady. It transpired that her name was "Sally" and she was the sisters' grandmother. I told them this, noting their surprise.

'This is your Gran, Sally.'

'She's telling me that she had a heart attack and crossed to the World of Spirit at the age of 78.'

Linda looked at her sister, then at me and nodded.

Sally impressed upon my inner consciousness that the girls had nothing to worry about. The fortune teller was wrong.

They looked immensely relieved. The tension fell visibly from their faces and they began to relax.

Then Sally made me aware that she wanted me to look directly at Carla and say that she loved her little boy, Jamie. Carla's face was an absolute picture.

She exclaimed, 'But my Gran never saw Jamie!'

'Not when she was on the earth, but she can him from where she is now.'

Carla smiled. 'We've nothing more to worry about, have we David?' she said.

'No,' I replied.

Sally began to step back. 'I'm going to leave your Gran's love with you,' I told the sisters.

Linda was overjoyed. I knew that Carla was feeling a little bit guilty about the anxiety she had provoked in her sister.

When they left, I was oh so tired! However, the satisfaction I had gained from being able to help them and from seeing their relaxed, smiling faces as we said goodbye was immense. Later that evening, I received a text message in which Carla and Linda re-iterated their thanks, told me that they were now convinced that there is an After Life and that when their mother does leave this earth, they will know that she has only gone before them to a better place.

I have come to realize that every day, every hour, every moment even, presents another lesson to be learnt in life. My experience with the sisters reinforced my strong sense of personal responsibility towards those who come to me for help. I know that I must never pass on information I receive from the Spirit World if I judge that it will cause distress to a client. I will disclose only that which will be of comfort.

Some weeks later, a Mrs. Wellans came to me for a private sitting. She wanted to communicate with her husband. *He* was anxious to communicate with *her* and gave me his full name, 'Albert William Wellans'.

After the communication had ended, we sat and chatted generally for a while and the information she imparted to me was of great interest – that she had consulted a Tarot reader near the Dock Road in Liverpool. 'She told me my first husband's first name and that he was suffering at the time. Then she said that he would be dead within a year.' Mrs Wellans paused, looking grave, then went on, 'She was right, he died in November, just six months after the reading.'

What Mrs Wellans said next sounded all-too-familiar.

'I used to lie awake at night thinking about that reading. When Al died, about eight of the girls from work went for readings to the same lady. Six out of the eight had the same message. One of the ladies was a spinster and the husband of another had died ten years previously. She'd never had a male friend since, let alone re-married. So the reader couldn't have been more wrong.' I looked at Mrs Wellans, she looked at me and spontaneously we both burst out laughing. Then she said, soberly, 'but that lady died.'

'Oh how awful,' I replied. 'Well, she's with her husband now.'

Mrs Wellans shook her head. 'No David, you misunderstand what I'm saying. It was the *Tarot* lady who died – she didn't see *that* coming!'

My belief is that we are all spirits within a human body which is the vehicle that enables us to live on this earthly plane. When the time comes, our spirit returns to the world from which it originated. The precise time at which this will happen cannot be known by Man.

Chapter 20

The Future Beckons

It had been a busy twelve months. The vast majority of my demonstrations had been very successful. People had warmed to me as a medium, and to my "psychic sidekick", Barry, the artist. But I was beginning now to feel the strain. Everything seemed to be a burden to me and my health was deteriorating. I felt disillusioned by everything and everyone around me. The immense negativity I felt towards my fellow human beings became unbearable. On the hair salon floor, I had to put on a front trying to appear happy and settled. However, I was going closer and closer to the edge of a dark abyss from which there would be no return. My staff at work were very supportive of me as they observed the change in me. In desperation I turned to June, my psychic friend, for advice. It was not the first time I had done so. One cold wet night, I journeyed over to her house where June immediately put the kettle on and began to talk to me.

'David, you have developed very, very quickly in the spiritual realm. Some mediums spend a lifetime developing and only reach half as far as you have done. You are open to the World of Spirit, but being so open has its drawbacks and your sensitivity is greatly heightened. When you are sad, you hit rock bottom; when you are happy your feet could leave the ground and it's important that you should be aware of this.'

I acknowledged that what June was saying was correct.

'I think it likely that you don't close down properly after clairvoyance, David,' she said.

'You see it's important to switch off completely. June advised me to have something to eat after a demonstration. She explained that the very human action of eating and digesting food would help to "ground" me. In addition, she thought that I was doing too many demonstrations which was having a draining effect on me, especially as I was working full-time in the salon.

She was beginning to sound like my mother. They always seem to know best, mothers do. Funny that, isn't it? But what is strange is that whenever my mother attempts to give me good advice, I always feel a little bit defiant, but it is different when June talks to me.

For some reason, I am more amenable to accept what she says. 'David, you will not be able to continue to give of your best at your demonstrations if you don't listen to me. Your job is physically demanding and your clairvoyance takes a huge amount of mental energy. Together, they take a lot out of you. That is why you feel as you do. Your body needs time to rest and recuperate. You are suffering from stress.'

I recognised that what June said was good advice. I thanked her profusely and went home, feeling much better.

Andrea and Barry were busy. Barry was at his computer whilst Andrea was catching up on her ironing.

'How did you get on at June's?' she asked hesitantly.

'I feel as if I have had a personality transplant,' I joked.

'Thank God for that!' Andrea teased.

Barry came into the room, his hands full of letters. 'How did you get on David?' he enquired.

'Great, I feel as if a weight has been lifted off my shoulders.'

Barry smiled. 'Thank goodness for that; now we might have a bit of a break from your mood swings.' It was only then that I realized the effect I had had on those closest to me.

Meekly, and to show my wish to make amends, I offered to put the kettle on.

I had been quite unaware how much my moods had affected my wife and my best friend, so great had been my preoccupation with my own problems. Since then, I have spoken to other mediums who have encountered similar problems as they have gone through the development process and then have been subject to the same kind of mood swings as I experienced. 'Heightening one's awareness' is how the process is usually described – in my case, it nearly cost me three shops full of customers and staff, one marriage, one mother and my best friend.

Sometimes, people will ask me if I am able to advise myself about the best course of action to take in a given situation in the same way as I am able to advise others. The answer is 'Yes, sometimes, but not all the time.' On this occasion, I resolved to take June's advice and cut down on the number of demonstrations I was giving. I had to acknowledge that I had been over-doing things for quite a long time, and then, to cap it all, I suddenly had an extra source of tension to deal with.

For twenty years, I had rented the premises in which my salon was situated. I had never actually met my landlord. Then, he contacted me out of the blue to ask if I would like to buy the premises. I was quite unprepared for this. Coming on top of the stress I was already suffering from, I felt unable to make an immediate decision. 'Could I have some time to think about it?' I hesitantly enquired of my landlord.

Since Jason came into my life, I have always consulted him about any major decisions I have to take. Having sought his opinion, I then speak to Andrea, Barry and my mum. I hold a sort of board meeting. On this occasion, Jason's advice was to buy the unit. The asking price was a large amount of money for me – hence my hesitancy – but Jason believed that it was worth it. He also told me that in twenty years, it would be worth two and a half times what I was being asked to pay now. Although I have absolute trust in Jason, this was a decision which could have far-reaching consequences for others besides myself – Andrea, Barry, all my staff – and so I knew I daren't make the wrong decision. At the back of my mind was the fear that it was my own subconscious mind which was telling me how to act, and that the advice was not coming from Jason at all. I was on the horns of a dilemma. Then I did something I have never done before: I asked Jason to give me a sign that it *was* he I had been communicating with. I knew he would not be offended at this because he would realize it was not him I doubted but myself. He told me that I would see three police cars when I was on my way to work the following morning. Many people might be expected to see three police cars on their way to work. My journey, however, takes me through open countryside where I see hardly any cars at all. It is only at the very end that there are any major roads. That morning – I saw three police cars! That was my decision made then! I should buy the unit.

Some weeks afterwards when arrangements were well advanced for the purchase, I was reminded that people sometimes exercise their free will by changing their minds. So I was disappointed to learn that the vendor had done just that and had given "back word" on the deal.

I expect it may be of interest to some of my readers to know whether I ever "read" for myself. The answer is "very, very seldom".

Immediately after I had definitely decided I was going to buy the shop, I had a visit from my great friend Jane. She had telephoned because she had not heard from me for a while and had been experiencing uneasy feelings about me. I apologized for not keeping in touch with her and explained that I had been very busy and that there were changes in the offing which were likely to take up even more of my time. She promptly offered to come to my home to give me a life reading. I should explain that this is when another medium talks to you, giving you direction and answers to any problems, both good and bad, on your journey ahead. I ought also to state that it is very rare indeed for me to seek guidance from other mediums, apart from June.

Jane and I sat in my dining room. The first thing she told me was that she was aware that I had "grown" spiritually, and would continue to do so.

Then she announced that I would travel abroad to give mediumship demonstrations. She mentioned America and India.

This filled me with amazement. 'I can't, Jane!' I burst out. 'What about my business, my salons?'

'Spirit will provide David. Everything will carry on without you. It will be business as usual. In addition, your first book will be published in the not-too-distant future. It will be a great success and there is more to come. There will be television appearances. You are going to be a very well-known man David. I realize this is difficult for you to believe now, but watch this space.'

I was speechless.

Then Jane began to talk about a problem connected with a rented property.

'Someone is renting a terraced house from you and they are in arrears with the rent,' she stated.

'That's correct,' I replied.

'Spirits are working on that situation. The problem will be resolved.'

I can see inner walls being removed, do you understand David?' Jane asked.

'Yes, we have decided to take over the unit next door. It becomes available after Christmas and we are going to take out the party walls and expand the floor space and working area.'

Next, Jane told me I would be having a holiday in France.

'Yes, that's next year. It's booked,' I confirmed.

Then she said, 'I feel you are worrying about how you will cope with your mediumship and your hairdressing. You fear that the two will clash and it will be impossible to do both, but they will come together and blend. You have no need to worry.'

'Bless you, Jane, and thank you,' I replied.

It was a great comfort to me to hear that it was going to be possible to combine these two activities. I've always enjoyed my work, but mediumship had come to the fore and I feared that one or other of these all-consuming interests would have to go. Finally, Jane disclosed that that her spirit guides were indicating that very soon, I would come to view my mediumship from a different angle. I could only wait and see if this would be the case.

June had once said to me, at an earlier sitting, 'Whenever you see a feather in your path, the spirits are telling you that your development has taken another step forward.' A few weeks after that reading, walking the half mile from my home to my local gym, I counted 48 feathers on the path in front of me. I remembered what June had said, and that is why I counted them. Shortly after this, I was, indeed, aware of a strengthening of my links with the Spirit World.

I turned my mind back to the present, with Jane, who was smiling and expressing the hope that what she had said was helpful and made sense to me.

I smiled back and thanked Jane again.

Scarcely had the words left my lips than I heard a woman's voice in my head saying, *Tell Jane it was Diana Dors, who appeared on the wall attempting to communicate with her whilst she was engaged in a private sitting.*

I repeated this, word-for-word, to Jane.

She gasped in surprise. 'David, I thought it was my imagination, but it *was* her then! She *was* trying to communicate. I had great difficulty in trusting my own psychic sensibilities!'

After Jane had gone I sat alone in my dining room, sipping a glass of red wine and contemplating what had been said during my reading. I reviewed the changes which had taken place in my life since I had begun to develop my gift two years previously. I had definitely become calmer and maybe a little more serious. I'd have described myself before these changes took place as "explosive" and "loud". I must admit I prefer my calmer self. It was as if my emotions had been "tweaked" during this period of time until I became extremely sensitive. It is a period which I refer to as my "spiritual attunement". Not long before, I had gone into a pet shop to buy some cold-water fish food. In one of the tanks, a little goldfish was floating on the surface of the tank. To my acute embarrassment, and without any warning, I burst into uncontrollable sobbing because the fish had crossed over into the World of Spirit. Thankfully, I have now gained more control over such overwhelming emotions.

My thoughts turned to one of my customers at the salon who is a member of the church situated near the salon. She came to hear that I am a medium and so decided to try to find out more about what I was doing. As I was blow-drying her hair, she stated baldly, 'David you are doing the devil's work, you are a disciple of evil.' My reply was simply, 'Rubbish!' 'I've always tried to help people in any way I can. I have a strong belief in God.' My customer fell silent. From that day to this, although I have blow-dried her hair many times since, she has never broached the subject again.

December was already upon us; the salons were absolutely packed full of perms, colours and cut and blow-dry customers all getting ready for their Christmas parties. I was drawing to the end of my diary of demonstrations. I was ready for a break.

Barry and I had been invited to lead a demonstration of mediumship and psychic art at the Spiritual Centre in Darwen. What was different about this demonstration was that we'd all been asked, after our demonstrations of clairvoyance, to take part in a 15-minute Christmas Concert to be held after the service. The concert would be staged by the Committee and the senior members of the Spiritual Centre. I discussed it with Barry and we decided that we would take part. The Bookings Secretary had asked us to put to together a three-minute sketch of our choice which would end the concert.

Two days before the service, Barry and I were still very vague as to what we were going to do. Finally, we decided to dress up as two old dears going to a spiritualist church to contact their husbands on the Other Side to wish them a Happy Christmas, but the two old dears would take a wrong turn on the way, then go in the wrong direction and end up in a Social Club where, after a few tots of "mother's ruin", they would get up on the stage and sing a song. We thought a suitable choice would be Michael Ball's version of *Let the Rivers Run*. We would mime to this and, as it's a lively song, the audience would be able to sing along, clap and dance. We could use our walking sticks as microphones. If nothing else it would provide a good laugh for the audience and end the event on a "high" for that year.

The day of the service arrived and Barry's diabetes was obviously going to be a problem. His blood sugar was fluctuating between 1.9 and 13. Anyone familiar with the disease will know how serious and disabling this can be. It plays havoc with the body. After work, he looked weak and dispirited. There was nothing else for it but for me to conduct the clairvoyance on my own and to do a solo version of our sketch. I felt so sorry for Barry who looked bitterly disappointed. But he conceded that he had no energy and would be unable to perform.

All those taking part in the clairvoyance demonstration had a successful evening, which was much appreciated by the audience. There was much laughter. When it came to my turn to go up on stage, I said a fervent prayer that I would be able to match the success of the other performers as I didn't want to disappoint the audience. Things went well. Then, just as I was about to finish, a man on the other side attracted my attention. He made me aware that his name was "Bill". He was smiling and holding a little girl, no older than about 20 months, who had her arms clasped tightly round his neck and her face pressed against the side of his head. I waited for him to indicate whom it was he wished to contact. He gestured towards an elderly lady, sitting on the front row of the audience.

'I'd like to come to you my dear,' I said. 'A gentleman, whose name is "Bill", has joined me from the World of Spirit. I believe he is your husband.'

A light of recognition came into the lady's eyes and she murmured, 'Yes,' very quietly.

'I will repeat what Bill says, word for word,' I went on. The lady nodded. Bill's actual words were, *Don't worry, love, our grand-*

daughter has come to me for Christmas. The child has come to me for Christmas.

There were astonished gasps from the audience. The lady covered her face with her hands to hide her emotion. After a brief space, she whispered, 'Yes, yes, I understand completely David. Thank you, so much.'

'Bill wants me to tell you, all of you, to have a lovely Christmas, the little girl's fine. I'll leave their love with you.'

'Thank you David, thank you,' the lady repeated.

The whole congregation seemed to be overcome with emotion. I thought my demonstration had come to its own conclusion so I decided to end it there.

I was so pleased that the evidence of the After Life I had been able to give was a sort of universal message for everyone in the hall, a message of hope and comfort for all who had lost a loved one. Nor was my solo concert turn an anticlimax. Despite the fact that it lasted only three minutes, it brought back memories of my Amateur Dramatics days. I was so elated at the end of it, I thought I deserved an Academy Award – well a cup of coffee and a biscuit, at least.

At the end of the evening, the lady to whom I had given the message which had affected everybody came over to thank me. She explained her granddaughter had been born with a number of health problems which she had struggled valiantly to overcome. Just a few days previously, she had lost her fight for survival and passed over into the World of Spirit. Her body still lay in the Chapel of Rest at the Children's Hospice where she had died. The old lady smiled. Her smile didn't hide her sadness.

'I can't wait to tell my daughter and son. It will bring them peace I'm sure. Thank you again, David.'

She took hold of my hand and squeezed it. I could feel my own eyes fill up with tears.

'If there was no life after death, it would not be possible for me to make contact in this way.'

She gave a little nod of agreement.

I've spoken before of the sense of satisfaction I feel when I have been able to bring comfort to someone who is grieving. In cases such as the one I have just described, this satisfaction is immense. I often receive profuse thanks from those to whom I have brought comfort, but as I constantly remind myself, I am merely the medium by which those in the Spirit World contact those on this Earth.

It is they who do all the work to ensure that their message is transmitted accurately and in such a way that it will convince their intended recipients.

Bill and his granddaughter and the Christmas audience in Darwen will remain in my memory for a long time. Another equally significant occasion occurred just recently – an occasion when I witnessed the inner peace experienced as a result of a communication from the Other World. Martin was one of my first spirit contacts. I have described how I encountered him, earlier in this book. His mother, Linda, has become a personal friend. She has been helping me in the compilation of this book, transcribing my words from a dictaphone onto computer. She had called at my house to collect the latest instalment and we fell into general conversation. There, suddenly, was Martin. I could see him clearly with my inner eye and greeted him aloud. By way of answer, Martin stuck up his thumb, making the universal gesture to indicate that things are "O.K.". Linda broke off what she was saying when I spoke to her son.

Then she remarked, 'David, ever since you first contacted Martin for me, I've wanted to ask him a question …'

Before Linda could get the question out of her mouth, Martin gave me the answer.

'Yes Linda, Martin *did* come into your bedroom on that night and he did sit on the edge of the bed. He's confirming this.'

Linda looked up and began to cry. 'I knew it was! I knew it was Martin! If he ever wants to come again he is welcome,' she exclaimed through her tears.

'He heard you Linda,' I replied.

It was obvious to me that the sense of peace in Linda's heart was immense. Her son had given her the answer to a question she had not even asked.

I should point out that it is much easier for a medium to relay a message from a loved one in the World of Spirit than it is to ask a spirit a question and receive a satisfactory answer. It is usually only after a number of communications with the same person in spirit that this is possible. The growing familiarity strengthens the link. In the early days of my mediumship, I invariably found that whenever I attempted to gain an answer from the World of Spirit in response to a question asked by a client, my own subconscious mind would step in and supply the answer. There are mediums who, having asked a question, will give as the answer the first thing that comes into their head. They believe that this first thought comes from the Spirit World and is the answer to the question just posed. My experience has taught me that although this is often the case, it is not always so. The help of a guide in the Spirit World is invaluable here. Whenever a client requests me to ask a question, I rely heavily on Jason and my other spirit guides to help me.

Barry, Andrea and I once went to watch a local medium demonstrate in a Country House near to where we live. During the demonstration, he turned his attention to a lady sitting several rows in front of us. He was apparently in touch with the woman's mother in the Spirit World. 'Your mother says you are at present converting a barn,' he said. The recipient of this message confirmed that this was so, then added, 'If you have my mother with you, ask her which room she insisted that I was to leave until last.' The medium frowned darkly. He snapped bluntly, 'Please be quiet, you are destroying my link with her!' The woman didn't say another word. I knew that the reason for his apparent rudeness was the difficulty in establishing and maintaining a link with the Other Side.

Those of you who attend demonstrations of clairvoyance or book themselves a one-to-one private sitting with a medium should be aware that it cannot be guaranteed that the medium will be able to contact a specific individual, or indeed anyone, on the Other Side. It should be understood that mediumship is a three-way communication – it involves the inquirer, the medium and the individual who has crossed over to the Higher Side of life.

It is a great help to a medium, particularly during a demonstration, if members of the audience whom he or she addresses will answer with a clear "yes" or "no". Some people attend psychic demonstrations purely to be entertained and do not wish to take part. If a medium approaches them, they will shy away and reject the medium's overture, refusing to listen to a message meant for them. I have given many a demonstration where members of an audience have destroyed their own links. Generally speaking, mediums do not ask questions of the audience, they work by making statements which the members of the public they address should understand or fail to understand. It is helpful to both if they answer clearly when offered information by a medium.

At a one-to-one sitting, a client should expect to receive some evidence of life after death. More often than not, an individual will book a private sitting with a medium because a loved one has died in the recent past and they hope to gain contact with that person through the medium. They are seeking comfort and proof of life after death, but more than anything, they want to be in contact with the person they have lost. However, the medium cannot guarantee that this person will "come through". Perhaps other family members in the Spirit World will manifest themselves to the medium with various messages for his or her client, but a medium has no power to "summon up" a departed soul. There is a wide misconception that mediums can "raise the dead". It should be remembered that those in the Spirit World can choose whether or not to seek contact with this world, in the same way as we can choose to contact them. The case of John, Sheila and Malcolm is an illustration of this.

Chapter 21

Epilogue

There are many people who think that mediums invariably use ouija boards, hold séances or dabble in black magic. They are mistaken. Usually, psychic spiritual abilities develop within the supersensitives of our world. Those who are psychic are usually unaware that they are any different from anyone else. Commonly, they believe that everyone has the same insight or the ability to communicate with people who are no longer on this Earth. Then, by chance – and it usually comes as a great surprise to them – they discover that these gifts have not been entrusted to the generality of mankind. An inevitable question for most "mediums" is – why? Or, why me? What is the reason for their gift?

I believe that the reason why God has given me, and others like me, the gift of Mediumship is so that we are able to offer reassurance to those whose loved ones have made the transition to the future life.

My whole concept of death has changed. It is impossible for me to believe that there is no life after death. If life on earth is all there is, how is it possible for me to contact the dead friends and relatives of those who have sought my help in contacting them? According to some people, when you die there is nothing and certainly no one there to contact. But that does not fit in with my experience, nor that of those who have had private sittings or have attended my public demonstrations.

It is over two years since I set foot on the spiritual path. Much has happened in that time and yet I feel that I am still at the start of a very exciting journey. The people I have met have played no small part in that journey and helped me to expand my self-awareness. We must not expect to progress on our own – we need the help of our fellow men. I therefore acknowledge my debt to all those I have encountered who have enabled me to take the first step, the second and the next, towards my destiny. I believe we have been placed on this Earth to extend a helping hand to those in any kind of need and, in return, we will receive help in our own time of trouble.

I am eager to continue my spiritual journey. I set out joyously...

The following are a few of the many testimonials that have been sent or given to David Traynor by grateful clients who have been comforted, encouraged and convinced by his spiritual gift.

Dear David,

Before the sudden death of my wife on 20th January 2004, I have to admit I was a sceptic about life after death.

Shortly after, I had the good fortune to meet you at a spiritual meeting which I attended with my daughter. You kindly agreed to give us a private reading at your home.

As a result of a number of private meetings with you, I am no longer a sceptic.

I am totally convinced that I have had contact with my wife through you and that life does in fact continue after death.

I am convinced by validation from my wife on facts and circumstances known only to ourselves.

The contact with my wife through you has greatly eased my sense of loss and has certainly given me a greater degree of peace of mind. I am also totally convinced that at some time there will be a new beginning with my wife.

Roy

Dear David,

We would like to thank you for taking the time and trouble to see us after our recent bereavement. You made us feel very welcome and were very comforting.

My mum was a big believer in the After Life and I have had the same interest as well. My dad Roy didn't disbelieve but didn't totally believe either. After visiting you he now has no doubt that there is an afterlife. Your readings were very accurate and you told us things that you couldn't possibly have known. Everyone was very shocked at the sudden death of my mum and my dad was totally devastated. They had been married since they were 19 and to be suddenly left on your own after nearly 50 years is a very big thing to take in but you helped him so much. After your first reading it was like a big weight had been lifted off his shoulders and he had more hope for the future, he knew that my mum was still around and knew what was happening and how he was feeling. This made him feel so much better. He takes great comfort to know that they will meet again some day. It hasn't been just the readings that you have given us, it's the time and patience that you've taken to explain everything, this is a special quality that not a lot of people have.

We'll never forget my mum but you have made the way forward for my dad so much easier to bear, for this we thank you,

Bev and Roy

We contacted David in the summer of 2004, to explore the idea that we would be able to contact our dad following his death from Cancer in 1990.

We had been to a number of different spiritual meetings, and although we did have contact with some members of our family, we were never fully satisfied that it was our dad.

Before actually meeting David he spoke to Julie on the telephone and even then, said that our dad was with him, he described him exactly as we would have known him, even down to the clothes he was wearing, a favourite grey jumper, and the fact that he was on crutches. Several months before his death he had broken his ankle.

The meeting was arranged, and David asked us to take several personal possessions of our dad's. When our Mum went to look for these, they were neatly laid out in a drawer. Bear in mind that our dad died in 1990, many of the items had not been looked at since. The fact that the items were on top of all the other items in the drawer gave us encouragement that something exciting may happen at our meeting.

During our meeting David gave us some very credible evidence that it was, in fact, our dad who was making contact. The way David described how he was sat on the sofa was our dad to a tee! To see David demonstrate how he saw our dad sat on the sofa was incredible!! At the very end of the meeting David shocked us both by stating our dad's full name as Francis Raymond Smethurst. Very few people knew his full name, as to everyone, he was simply known as Ray. This is what really settled it for us both, and knowing David had contacted our dad gave us great comfort and put our minds at rest, that our dad was OK and was at peace in the Spirit World.

signed Michael Smethurst   *Julie Smethurst*

Haydock, St Helens, Merseyside

MY EXPERIENCE OF A PSYCHIC MEDIUM

a.k.a. DAVID TRAYNOR

By Shirley Butterworth (née Twist)

I have known David Traynor since 1985 but only discovered he had psychic talents in September 2002, about six months after my identical twin sister Angela died. I was visiting David and his wife one weekend when he mentioned he had been to a spiritualist meeting and that a psychic medium had singled him out to tell him he was psychic too. David continued to tell me he had been sensing spirits around his clients in the salon and that the spirits were giving him messages to pass onto their loved ones. I was quite sceptical and even laughed about it for a while. I have always had big doubts about psychic mediums, especially the ones you see on TV. Quite a few of my friends have seen mediums and raved about them but I have always though that the evidence was far too generic and could apply to almost anyone in certain circumstances. I'm the kind of person who needs specific and indisputable evidence before I can believe in spirits giving messages to human beings.

At this time, David knew I wasn't ready to listen to any spiritual messages or evidence and didn't push me into having a reading. A further six months passed and it was March 2003 (just coming up to a year since Angela died). I was visiting the Traynors again, when I challenged David to give me a reading – truly believing that he wasn't going to tell me anything of any consequence. He sat me down at a small table and firstly asked for a piece of jewellery I was wearing. I gave him a ring; he said not to tell him anything about it so I didn't. David then proceeded to tell me there were spirits in the room and started to describe them. He gave me evidence of my grandparents (neither of whom he had ever met, nor of whom I had ever really spoken) and of rooms and objects in their house (which he had never visited). Of course, I was intrigued but still thinking maybe I'd spoken of them more than I thought.

Then David did a Tarot reading for me, which was unusual as he described the cards and their meaning with the cards face down, only turning them over when he had finished the reading. A lot of the information he gave me from the cards was stuff he already knew about me; past, present and future, so I couldn't be sure of his skills at this point, except to say the turnout of the cards was accurate each time.

Two days later, I accompanied David and his wife on a trip to the DIY centre. As we were sat in the car prior to going into the store, out of the blue David asked me some questions about specific recent events in my life, of which I was certain he knew nothing. Then he told me that my sister had told him these details as evidence and she wanted to come through to give me a message – wanted to let me know she was okay; that she knew I'd been worrying about her since she passed over. During the same day, David told me that my sister's dog, Judith, had been ill – her back legs had gotten weak and she was suffering with them. I eventually confirmed this evidence three months later when I spoke to my brother-in-law.

On returning home from that weekend, I realised I had been deeply saddened and even mildly depressed since my sister's death but after seeing David and hearing the messages from my sister I felt like a heavy weight had been lifted off my shoulders.

In July 2003 I visited David again. This time I met his spiritual mentor, Jane. She said she could instantly feel

my sister's spirit around me. David asked if I had a photo
of Angela to give to Jane, and to give it to her face down,
which I did. Jane proceeded to give me evidence of my
sister's presence by referring to specific incidents in our
past. I had never met Jane before and so I was certain
that she knew nothing of those events. Doubtfully I
thought, "Has David told her these things?", but I knew he
wasn't aware of them either. Then without looking at the
down-turned photo she described the scene in the picture,
which was exactly right, even down to explaining that my
sister was on a company boat trip around the Isle of Wight.
I was quite amazed as the sceptic in me couldn't quite
believe what she had just told me.

The next time I saw David was a weekend in
October 2003. I was with my husband, Mike... now he is a
bigger sceptic than I am. We had been out for the evening
and had a few drinks, talking and laughing about David
being 'psycho'. On our return a slightly inebriated David
tried to give Mike some proof of his psychic abilities but the
only thing he really came up with was something about
'eagles'. Again I was quite certain I had never told David
this, but my husband's favourite American Football team
is... the Philadelphia Eagles. I have to say that my husband
still thinks either I told David about that or that David has
some kind of a telepathic ability. Some people are hard to
convince!

On this same weekend, David told me that a friend
of mine (who he specifically named) was to find themselves
very ill. Within three months I heard the sad news that
this person had cancer.

Well, as my wedding plans progressed towards April
2004, I didn't have time to see David again until he came out
to our wedding on a Caribbean island called St. Kitts.

Towards the end of our holiday David sat me and another friend down. He continued to describe accurately events in my friend's life that I was aware of but I know he was not. David then told me that he knew my sister was with me on the day of the wedding. He said he could see her walking down the aisle behind me like a bridesmaid, which is what she would have been had she still been alive. To provide evidence of this message he told me the details of a disagreement I'd had with my husband a few months prior. Needless to say, I have had so much personal proof of David's abilities that I have to believe he is truly psychic, although I still want him to give enough evidence to my husband so that he will believe too.

I now reside in the USA but in September 2004 I returned home to the UK and stayed with David and his wife. During this visit I had only one piece of evidence from David… it was about my friend who had cancer. David told me that my friend wouldn't live out the year. Regrettably, I wish David hadn't been right this time but sadly, my friend died in November, 2004.

I also went to three of David's psychic/spiritual meetings in September, two of which were astounding. The evidence he gave to people, their reactions to it, and my questioning of them afterwards all lead me to say he is one of the best mediums I have ever seen or heard of, on TV or face-to-face.

I would like to believe that David finally recognised his psychic abilities because my sister sought him out from the Spirit World so that she could still communicate with me. Wishful thinking? I think not!

Shirley Butterworth

A Bridge to Angels

David Traynor is preparing his second book which will be published later this year. It will be entitled *A Bridge to Angels* and relates the true life stories of the sad loss of loved ones and of those here on the Earth plane eager to make contact with family members in the World of Spirit. With his extraordinary ability, David succeeds in bringing hope and love from the other side which, in turn, gives comfort and peace of mind to the many bereaved relatives and friends left behind.

David Traynor is the bridge to *your* angels.

A Bridge to Angels
ISBN 1-900734-38-9

www.davidtraynor.com

◇JADE◇
JADE PUBLISHING LIMITED